# The
# Missing
# Generation

by

Robert L. Bast

co-published by

**REFORMED CHURCH IN AMERICA**
New York, NY

&

**CHURCH GROWTH, INC.**
Monrovia, CA

To the memory of my parents

Sena Gerding Bast
1905 - 1939

Henry Bast
1906 - 1983

# CONTENTS

# Acknowledgments

My interest in how the church could effectively reach young adults began when I was the pastor of a congregation which made an intentional decision to focus on this age group. During our years in that ministry, we did reach some of those individuals and learned a few things along the way. Later I joined the staff of the Reformed Church in America with responsibility for directing the ministry of evangelism. Knowing the importance of reaching the young unchurched furthered my interest in the baby boom. We later developed a seminar on that theme, and it became clear that many people shared a concern for reaching this generation.

After one presentation of the seminar for Church Growth, Inc., Win Arn encouraged me to write a book on this subject. Eugene Heideman, the Reformed Church's secretary for program, urged me to accept this challenge. My growing interest threatened to become a constant pre-occupation. A survey of the field failed to turn up what I was looking for — a broad overview of the baby boom generation and a comprehensive approach for a church that wanted to reach them. Consequently, I decided to attempt this project.

Suzanne Braden, a colleague and friend in the United Methodist Church, arranged for me to attend a conference on "Reaching for the Baby Boom." That event confirmed my decision and broadened my knowledge. Colleagues and friends who knew of my interest began to send me material, and my files grew thicker. Finally, writing began.

I am indebted to many people for their help and assistance. I owe a special thanks to the staff of Church Growth, Inc., particularly to Win Arn for his support and encouragement, to my friend Bob Orr with whom I have talked over and jointly taught much of this material, and to Charles Arn, my gracious and supportive editor. I am deeply indebted to Dr. Donald Luidens, associate professor of sociology at Hope College, for his kindness in offering helpful comments on the opening chapters, and to my colleagues Kenneth Bradsell and John Paarlberg for reviewing parts of this material. I also wish to express appreciation to my son, Robert J. Bast, who went over the manuscript and helped me understand how this material might appear to the people of his generation. I owe much to my wife Jan, for her faithful support as well as for her valuable suggestions for improvement. Special thanks are due to my efficient secretary, Kathleen Koschal, who processed this material through many revisions, and took over other tasks so that I had time to write.

To each I gratefully acknowledge my debt.

# Introduction

This is a book about evangelization. The use of that term does not imply a rejection of the word "evangelism." "Evangelism" is a good and beautiful word which means "to bring good news." Our world can use all the good news it can get, and evangelism will always be an essential task and an appropriate term.

Yet, it cannot be denied that many people are uncomfortable with the term "evangelism." For some, it conjures up images of methods and practices which are highly suspect. To others, it suggests engaging in tasks which feel inappropriate or raises guilt about an aspect of the Christian life which has been ignored. Many people have negative feelings about the word.

That is part of my reason for choosing to use the term "evangelization," but only part. I use it in the hope that this word will help us look at the task of evangelism in a new way. Perhaps it will help us remember that Christian witness begins with actions, not words. It may serve as a reminder that the evangelizing task is a process rather than an event. It may even lead us to approach the task with appropriate humility, as fellow strugglers rather than experts with answers.

Some people say there is no difference between the terms. They may be right. But for me, just now, evangelization seems to be a good choice. It is a new term reminding me that we need to go about a timeless task in a fresh new way.

Before we launch out, it may be helpful to identify several assumptions which lie behind the material presented in this book.

First, evangelization is a priority for the church. One can hardly escape that conclusion if the New Testament is our model. We do well to recognize that the New Testament most often presents evangelization not as an expected duty, but rather as a natural response to a life-transforming event. One of the rich images the Bible uses for coming to Jesus Christ is that of being invited to a bountiful banquet. If we have been fed at God's table, it is hard to imagine being content to satisfy our own hunger without being concerned for other hungry people. Those who have found in Jesus Christ a source of peace, joy, and hope for their lives will be eager to share that gift with the world.

A second assumption is that evangelization is the responsibility of the church. To be sure, the church carries out its work through individual members, but evangelization is not simply one individual relating to another individual, but rather it is the Christian community reaching out to the world. The whole church is involved in evangelization.

A third assumption is that evangelization is most effective when it is directed to specific groups of people. While some might object that this is to limit the Great Commission, that is not its intent. Evangelization springs from a desire to reach all people, yet the church that is effective in evangelization is one that has identified certain groups to which its ministry effort will be specifically addressed. These will be people who have certain characteristics in common, and who can be found in significant numbers in the ministry area of the congregation. Win Arn suggests, in his *Growth Report*, that such "target group evangelism" is a secret to effective evangelization and growth for churches in the 1990s. [1]

A fourth assumption is that evangelization is most effective when it identifies and addresses the concerns, needs, and interests of people. The implication is that we need to know the people we are seeking to evangelize. Our concern may lead us to learn more about them in order to understand their needs, to spend time with them, and to listen to them so that we may provide ministry that is responsive to their needs. Following that, a church can identify its strengths, analyze its present membership, study its community, and then develop a plan for evangelization in light of these realities.

A fifth assumption is that evangelization is most effective when it reaches out to those whom God has prepared to respond. This has been described by church growth authorities as the "principle of receptivity." The image is that of sowing seed where the ground is fertile. Jesus' parable of the sower (Mark 4:1-8) points out the hope of an abundant harvest: "multiplying thirty, sixty, or even a hundred times" (verse 8).

This seems to be the strategy the apostle Paul followed on his missionary journeys. He often directed his ministry toward those who were called the "God fearers." These were people in the Gentile world who had come to believe in the God of Abraham and Sarah, Isaac and Rebekah, and Jacob and Rachel. They had come that far, but seemed to be waiting for more. When Paul told them about Jesus, they were prepared to believe. Similarly, in carrying out a ministry strategy, the church should be sure to engage people whose lives suggest the probing touch of God.

Our purpose in this book is to help congregations who wish to explore effective ministry with the "Baby Boom" generation. Many of these young adults are missing from our churches. In order to reach them, we need to understand who they are and recognize why many have chosen not to be involved with the church. We will also want to consider why some are making their way back, and to explore what needs to happen in congregations which hope to include them.

I am not a sociologist, and do not claim to be an expert in this field, but I have read as much as I can about the baby boom generation. To that reading I add my own experiences in three decades of ministry and the observations which have come from consulting with scores of churches and talking with hundreds of pastors.  From that I have attempted to distill what I think will be useful to those who wish to reach the baby boom.  If the church takes seriously the task of evangelizing America, it needs to begin with this generation.

---

[1] *Win Arn Growth Report #30.*  Church Growth, Inc., Monrovia, CA.

# CHAPTER ONE

# The Baby Boom Phenomenon

The birth rate in the United States, and in the western world as a whole, has been generally declining for nearly 200 years. It is still declining. One great exception to this general trend is the unprecedented "baby boom" which followed World War II. It might have been anticipated that with the world returning to stability following the war, and service personnel returning home, the number of births would show a dramatic increase. Sociologists expected that the birth rate increase would last for several years. In Europe, in fact, that is pretty much what happened.

In the United States (and Canada) it was a different story. After the U.S. birth rate peaked in 1947, with one-third more births than in 1945, the birth rate dropped back for three successive years. But then, after 1950, it took off again, showing an increase each year, and in 1954, registering four million births for the first time. Year after year, in spite of demographic projections to the contrary, babies kept coming in record numbers. Indeed, the peak year for births in the United States was 1957. Between the years 1946 and 1964, some seventy-five million babies were born in the United States. It was the greatest birth boom in modern history.

## A MASSIVE GENERATION

Those who share birth years from 1946-1964 make up the "baby boom generation." There are now about seventy-seven million people in this group within the United States. This represents approximately half of all adults, and nearly one third of the total United States population.

During the period of the baby boom, an average of nearly four million births occurred each year, and for eleven consecutive years, from 1954 through 1964, topped that number. It is interesting that after 1964, when the boom ended, America would not register another year with four million births until 1989, when births just topped that figure. To help put into perspective the significance of these numbers, here are the numbers of births for the United States in recent decades:

| | | |
|---|---|---|
| 1930 - 1939 | - | 24 million |
| 1940 - 1949 | - | 32 million |
| 1950 - 1959 | - | 40 million |
| 1960 - 1969 | - | 35 million |
| 1970 - 1979 | - | 33 million |
| 1980 - 1989 | - | 37 million |

What makes these figures remarkable is the realization that the parents who were born in the 1920s and 1930s were a relatively small generation, and yet they were primarily responsible for the huge number of children born in the baby boom. In contrast, the vast numbers of people born during the baby boom years have not had sufficient children to replace themselves.

A comparison of marriage and family patterns in the 1950s with today helps to put this in perspective. From 1940 to 1957, the fertility rate for women aged 20-24 nearly doubled, while the median age of first birth fell from 23 to 21.4. During the 1950s, more than half of all first time brides were in their teens, and half of those had a child before they turned twenty. By 1986, in contrast, the median age for women at their first marriage had passed 23. The figures in the 1950s are significant because the younger a woman was at marriage, the greater the number of children she would be likely to have.

The greatest impact of the baby boomers came as a result of their sheer number. For twelve straight years, from 1952 to 1964, the number of children entering kindergarten exceeded the number graduating from high school by an average of 1.5 million per year. This was an educational nightmare. No one was prepared for it. It led to overcrowded classrooms, split shifts, and thousands of mobile units lined up on playgrounds, while harried school boards scrambled to build additional facilities in order to catch up.

This skyrocketing birthrate led to a phenomenon that occurred in a number of churches as the baby boom moved into the school age. Since the church is often slower to react than other institutions, many churches "caught up" too late. It was just about the time the baby boom began to finally slow down that numbers of churches got around to building educational units for all the children who would be coming. Due to the time interval between planning and construction, such churches often saw their educational buildings being dedicated just about the time their Sunday school enrollments began to plummet.

Landon Y. Jones has written a classic work on the baby boom generation.[1] His book is an indispensable aid to understanding this phenomenon. In describing the baby boom generation, Jones uses the wonderful image of a python swallowing a pig. Get a picture of that in your mind, and you will have a vivid sense of the effect produced by the baby boom. Society is the python, and the baby boom generation the pig. It's not hard to understand that when a pig is swallowed by a python it is an uncomfortable experience for both. American society has had considerable difficulty "swallowing" the baby boom generation. For the most part, it has been unable to understand this generation, predict its behavior, or accept its uniqueness. The baby boomers' difficulty adjusting to American society can be vividly recalled by anyone who remembers the 1960s.

The figure of the pig in a python is helpful in illustrating another point. As the pig makes its journey through the body of the python, the bulge created continues to be evident. Similarly, the impact of the baby boom generation has been felt since its arrival. It continues to be felt today, and its effect will remain until the last of the generation passes from history sometime in the second half of the twenty-first century.

From the time of its arrival, the baby boom has strongly affected American society. "At every stage in their lives the baby boomers change the nature of the life stage they enter, and force the nation to devote extraordinary attention to the problems and needs of people in that age group." [2] Evidence of that is seen in all the attention being given today to "the middle-aging" of America, now that the oldest baby boomers are in their forties.

Another descriptive image for the baby boom is that of waiting in line. When all those children began to arrive in the late 1940s, the 1950s, and continuing into the 1960s, their numbers were not anticipated. As a result, there was not enough space in the nurseries of the hospitals in which they were born. There were not enough pediatricians to take care of them. As they grew older, there was inadequate school space to accommodate them, too few college facilities to educate them, insufficient jobs waiting as they moved into society, and not enough promotions available to accommodate their desire to move up the ladder.

As the future looms on the horizon, there is fear that the government programs to which they contribute through taxation will not meet their own needs. (Seventy percent of baby boomers believe that the social security system will not be available to accommodate their basic needs in retirement.) Already America is seeing signs of the coming "age wave" that will wash across the country. In 1983, for the first time in history, there were more Americans over age 65 than under age 18. In the coming decades, baby boomers will find inadequate pension plans to supplement their income, too few retirement communities and nursing homes to take care of them in old age, and probably not enough cemetery space in which they can be buried.

As we consider the unique qualities of these adults born between 1946 and 1964, think about your own church at the same time, and the likelihood of your congregation being able to reach and minister to these men and women.

## A UNIQUE GENERATION

In addition to their sheer numbers, other factors make the baby boom generation different from other generations. For one thing, they are highly educated. About half of all baby boomers have attended college and approximately one quarter are college graduates. That makes them the most educated generation in American history. That fact is not likely to change. The number of college graduates in a single year peaked at 969,000, with the class of 1984. That means the baby boomers will remain America's most educated generation.

All that education continues to affect the way members of this generation act. Highly educated people . . .

- are more sophisticated in their methods
- tend to make rational decisions
- like making comparisons
- are less brand loyal
- recognize and appreciate quality
- value saving
- make independent decisions.

The baby boomers are unique in the degree to which they share values and attitudes. One reason they are so much alike is because of common life experiences. The vast majority were raised in the suburbs. In fact, it could be said they *created* the suburbs, or at least that the suburbs were created for them. Parents moved out of the cities to the safe and spacious world of suburbia, where their children grew up on interchangeable streets and were raised in houses that looked alike. This pervasive sameness "may have provoked the drive for individualism and the tolerance of diversity that distinguishes the baby boom from its parents and grandparents today." [3]

The baby boom is unlike other generations in its self-understanding. This is a generation that believes in its uniqueness. They feel they are like no other generation. They have become accustomed throughout their lives to having products designed especially for them. They have grown used to, and continue to insist on, a wide variety of choices and options, and want them all to be of high quality.

We have been discussing the uniqueness of this generation, and should perhaps add a few qualifying statements. Attempting to characterize an entire generation, one made up of 77 million people, is risky if not foolhardy. One can only do so by painting with broad strokes. We are dealing with patterns and general characteristics, and that may be unfair to a group which prizes individuality. Yet, it is possible to point out common qualities which are characteristic of baby boomers, and that too is part of their uniqueness.

We also must understand that within the baby boom generation some observers identify two groups. They are described as "the first wave" (born between 1946-1954) and "the second wave" (born between 1955-1964). The break which divides the groups is not precise, but a fairly even span of years encompasses each group. We will not always take pains to separate the two groups, but we do need to keep in mind that some variations seem evident between older and younger baby boomers.

One difference is that first wave boomers tend to be better off financially than their younger brothers and sisters. Three factors come into play here. First, older baby boomers entered the market place at a time when the economy was on an upward swing. Jobs and salary increases were more available to them than to their younger colleagues. Second, many of the first wave were able to buy a house before property values began escalating in the early 1970s. One of the great problems for younger baby boomers is the problem of affordable housing. Third, the first wave are ten years further in their careers and therefore should be ahead financially.

Another difference is that older boomers were more shaped by the events of the 1960s than their younger brothers and sisters. With the caution that these are generalizations, we offer what seem to be some patterns. First wave baby boomers tend to have a strong social conscience and more liberal views on many issues. They are likely to be more idealistic, and are therefore perhaps more disenchanted. Younger boomers are often more conservative.

Some would say they tend to be more material-istic, as well. If that is the case, it may well be a result of their having less. They have certainly had a harder time economically than did those born between 1946 and 1954.


## AN ACCESSIBLE GENERATION

Now that we have taken a brief look at this generation, it is time to consider why we should spend time dealing with this group:

*There Are So Many of Them.*

Anyone concerned about evangelization will have a deep yearning to reach them. How can we ignore 77 million people — half of all adults? If, like Jesus, we have compassion for the multitudes who are so often harassed and helpless (Matthew 9:34), we cannot ignore the huge number of people who make up the baby boom generation. The sheer number of them is, in itself, a reason for a specific focus and an intentional plan. To evangelize America, the church must learn how to reach baby boomers.

*Many Are Missing from Our Churches.*

A nationwide study conducted by *People* magazine found that only 11 percent of baby boomers say they regularly attend a church or synagogue.[4]
I have no way to validate those figures. They are in contrast to the Gallup poll, which indicates a much higher level of involvement. Gallup issued a recent report on church

membership giving the results of a 1989 survey which asked people if they are a member of a church or synagogue. According to Gallup, among those aged 18 to 29, 61% said yes, and for those 30 to 49, the number was 68%. The national average was 69%.[5]

Those numbers seem impossibly high. Granted, membership and attendance figures can be far apart, but even so, if the poll is accurate, it must be assumed that there are vast numbers of people who claim they belong to a church — perhaps because they were once baptized — but who by any objective measurement would be considered unchurched.[6]

A more intensive study which has evoked considerable interest was sponsored by the Lilly Endowment. Carried out by sociologist Wade Clark Roof and researcher William McKinney, the study reports that approximately two-thirds of the baby boom generation have dropped out of religious participation for a period of two years or more. Only about 40 percent of the dropouts have returned to church.[7]

If that is correct, it appears that of the 77 million baby boomers, about 26 million were raised in the church and remain active. About 52 million have been outside the church for all or part of their lives. Approximately 21 million of them have found their way into the church. That results, in round numbers, in 47 million in the church, and 30 million outside. *It is this 30 million who are the "missing generation."*

Roof and McKinney conclude that the single greatest reason for membership decline in so many American churches is the failure to retain and reach the baby boom generation. That failure also accounts for the "graying" of the church, an appropriate expression in these times when in many churches, and even in some denominations, the average age of adult members has now passed fifty.[8]

We focus on the baby boomers because they are missing from our churches. Like a shepherd who has lost a sheep, a woman who has lost a coin, a father who has lost a son, we cannot rest until they are found (Luke 15).

*There is Evidence of Their Receptivity*

It has long been recognized that life-changes ("transition events") increase the probability of church involvement for people. Historically, people begin attending church in greater numbers after getting married, and especially after having children. Also, people are more likely to be active in a church as they move toward middle age. All of these factors are at work in the lives of great numbers of baby boomers, and one would expect to see an increased rate of participation in that group now. That appears to be happening, but it was by no means certain. The behavior of baby boomers has been notoriously difficult to predict, and a question still being debated by sociologists is whether boomers will conform to predictable expectations of mid-life behavior or whether they will force a re-evaluation of those expectations. While that question has yet to be answered, we can report that the expectation of greater church involvement seems on the way to being realized. The Roof-McKinney study reports that baby boomers are attending church in increasing numbers. "The researchers found that 40 percent of older baby boomers, those born between 1946 and 1954, said they were regularly attending worship services last year. Only 33 percent of this same generation reported regular church attendance in the 1970s."[9]

The reported 25 percent increase in church attendance is true of the older baby boomers, among whom more have experienced the life changes mentioned earlier. This suggests that life changes are having their predictable effect. That is reason for hope. In an article on this subject in the *New York Times*, Peter Steinfels adds this comment: "Although those born before 1955 attend religious services in higher numbers than do younger members of the generation, the younger group has actually been found to hold more traditional religious attitudes. And as younger members of the baby boom generation start having families, the return to organized religion may occur even more rapidly."[10]

This, too, gives reason for hope. Most baby boomers are still under age 35, and 40 million of them will reach age 40 in the decade of the 1990s. That alone is no guarantee the upswing will continue. Boomers have never hesitated to turn away from institutions which did not meet their needs, and we cannot take their return to church for granted.

It is not simply life stage that is bringing baby boomers back to church. *Christianity Today* magazine identified several other reasons for their return:  depression, unreal-

ized expectations, overextension, disenchant-
ment; "post-crash conversions" (in the wake of
the 1987 stock market crash), social activism, a
new openness to institutions; a need for
commitment, and a hunger for companion-
ship.[11]

Another evidence providing hope is an
indication of renewed openness to the church,
and an increased interest in spiritual values.
Gallup's 1988 study of the "Unchurched
American" indicated that 58 percent of those
who are unchurched are open to involvement.
That is the percentage of individuals who
answered "yes," "perhaps," or "possibly" to the
question: "Could there be a situation where
you could see yourself becoming a fairly active
member of a church now?" Ten years earlier,
in a previous study, Gallup found that 52
percent indicated a similar degree of openness.

Researcher George Barna has written a
paper entitled "Seven Trends Facing the
Church in the 1990s."[12] The first trend Barna
predicts is that church membership will grow.
Among the reasons he gives — some of which
we have already discussed — is that religion is
assuming a more important place in the lives
of Americans. "Since 1982, the proportion of
adults who claim that religion is 'very
important' in their lives has jumped nearly 20
percent — with much of that increase a result
of the renewed interest in religion among baby
boomers."

Given all this, we can safely conclude
that a focus on evangelizing 25 to 45-year-olds
is appropriate, for the time is right, and they
are interested.

*Many Respond When Churches Reach out to Them.*

No doubt there are many churches throughout the country which have learned from their own experience that this is true. Perhaps the best known of them is Willow Creek Community Church, in South Barrington, Illinois, whose story has been featured in *Time* magazine.[13]

What makes Willow Creek unusual is that from its inception in 1975, it was designed for baby boomers. "The prime market . . . is those 'unchurched Harrys,' 25 to 45-year-old professionals who have become disenchanted with the stodgy ritual and sanctimoniousness of many traditional churches . . . Weekend services are primarily intended to attract this group into the church."

Before the church was started, founding pastor Bill Hybels conducted an extensive survey in the community to find out people's attitudes about the church. Worship services were then planned in response to what the survey revealed. For example, one of the reasons people gave for not attending church was that the church is always asking for money. As a result, Willow Creek began the practice of announcing to visitors at each service that they are guests, and are not expected to put any money in the offering.

The services at Willow Creek continue to respond to surveys which indicate that baby boomers resent services which are boring and predictable, and are looking for those relevant to their lives. Willow Creek is reaching baby boomers: with weekend services averaging around 12,000 people, Willow Creek has become, according to *Time*, the second largest Protestant congregation in America. If the experience of Willow Creek is an accurate indication, when churches identify the baby boom as the group they intend to reach, and when they plan their ministry to respond to the needs and concerns of this generation, they will very likely experience positive results.

1 Landon Y. Jones, *Great Expectations, America and the Baby Boom Generation* New York: Bellantine Books, 1980. (Statistical information in this chapter is taken from this resource unless otherwise noted.)

2 Jones, *Great Expectations, America & the Baby Boom Generation* p. 1

3 Paul C. Light, *Baby Boomers* New York: W.W. Norton and Company, 1988. p. 111.

4 Quoted in "The Small Group Newsletter." *Discipleship Journal.* Issue 42, 1987. p. 41.

5 "Emerging Trends" Princeton Religion Research Center, February, 1990.

6 Gallup reports attendance patterns for ages 25 to 29 at 35 percent and for ages 30-49 at 41 percent in 1988, compared to a national average of 42 percent.

7 Reported in the Louisville, Kentucky, *Courier-Journal*, April 22, 1990.

8 Win and Charles Arn, "Are You Ready For The Age Wave ?", *Leadership*, Fall, 1990.

9 Reported in the *Grand Rapids Press*, November 25, 1989, and based on an article by Don Lattin in the *San Francisco Chronicle*.

10 *New York Times*, January 6, 1990.

11 *Christianity Today*, October 6, 1989.

12 Edward E. Moughman, editor, *National and International Religion Report.*

13 *Time* magazine, March 6, 1989, p. 60.

# CHAPTER TWO

# The Development of the Baby Boom Generation

Now that we have made a case for evangelizing the baby boom, we need to take time to get to know them.

With any generation, two primary ingredients go into the makeup of personality. They are the family (the parents, the household) in which the child is reared and the environment or society in which the child is raised. In learning more about baby boomers, it is helpful to look first at their parents and then at what was happening in society during the shaping years of childhood and adolescence. As with all of us, what happened during the year of our birth is not nearly as important as the events which took place during the years in which we grew up.

Let us compare three generations in twentieth century America, beginning with the grandparents of the baby boomers. Most grandparents of baby boomers were born between 1900 and 1920, and most grew up and entered adulthood without an abundance of material possessions. Many of them were immigrants or the children of immigrants. Nearly all of them knew hardship as a way of life. For many, a world war dominated the memory of childhood. They entered adulthood to witness a depression and a second world war. For most of them, life could be characterized by the expression "tough times." The values they developed had to do with the way they experienced life. They understood that life would be hard, sacrifices would be necessary, and happiness was not at all certain. They passed these values on to their children, the parents of the baby boomers.

The parents of most baby boomers were born between 1920 and 1940. Baby boomer parents had the reality of what they were taught by their parents confirmed in their own childhood and adolescence. For them, childhood memories include the Great Depression and World War II. They have a strong recollection of rationing, and remember hardships and the sacrifices that were demanded in the period between 1930 and 1945.

When this generation had children, the economic and social values their parents had taught them, which had been reinforced in their own shaping years, were passed on to their children. Like their parents, they preached that happiness is not certain, that life is hard, and that sacrifices are necessary. They talked about saving for a rainy day, and not buying until you could afford it. They remembered being and doing without, and the experiences of their growing up tended to confirm these attitudes and instill them as values.

After World War II, the world changed dramatically, and baby boom parents changed along with it. The economy mushroomed, money began to flow, all kinds of goods became available, and America discovered easy credit. Parents began to live by different standards, and found themselves preaching values and ethics which they had grown up believing but were no longer practicing.

Here is one key to understanding the baby boom generation: those principles taught by their parents about thrift, sacrifice, self-denial, hardship of life, and the uncertainty of happiness were not seen or validated in their growing up. It is always difficult to believe that which is denied by your own experience or by the evidence you have seen. As a result, baby boomers began to be unsure of, and even to question, some of the values of their parents. When that happened, it became probable they would reject other things they had been taught as well. And so it happened. Baby boomers dismissed their parents' values in the areas of hard work, material success, and competition. This was one factor in the eventual development of "counter-culture" values, which involved the challenging of traditional values. Permeated with this spirit, many baby boomers determined to chart their own courses and to do it in their own way. They resolved that they would not be like their parents.

A contrast can be developed around the attitude toward credit in these three generations. For the most part, the grandparents of baby boomers did not have, or even know of, credit. They saved until they could afford to buy. Most of them never had a charge card or paid for any purchase on an installment plan. Some of them would not even buy a house unless they could pay for it in cash.

The parents of baby boomers, for the most part, did have credit and used it. I imagine, however, that many of them used it hesitantly, perhaps even guiltily, and were quick to pay charges when they came due. The baby boomers themselves have only known a world of easy credit. They use it easily and naturally, and consider finance charges part of life. In each generation, the attitude and use of credit result not only from its availability, but from shaping influences in childhood.

## EARLY LIFE INFLUENCES

*Unparalleled Prosperity*

Following the Second World War, America entered a great economic boom, which lasted nearly three decades. During the childhood and youth of the baby boomers, goods were plentiful, markets were expanding, income was rising, credit was available, and freewheeling spending was everywhere.

Grandparents, who had been unable to give their own children many material goods during the decades of depression and war, could now lavish gifts upon grandchildren. Parents, who had been forced to do without for much of their own childhood, could make up for it in part through the goods they showered on their children. Children were key beneficiaries of this unparalleled prosperity as they were the recipients of a wealth of gifts and attention. "The affluence of the 1950s gave young baby boomers the notion that just about everything was in their grasp."[1]

The baby boom children were their parents' pride. Landon Jones points out a prevailing attitude in parents of the baby boomers: "This generation of Americans enshrined them. European visitors joked knowingly about how well American parents obeyed their children. American parents did seem to be making their kids their religion."[2] Children's needs came first, and they were at home in the world of the newest and the best.

That children are to be treated as special also came to be emphasized through the child-rearing theories being advocated, in particular by Benjamin Spock. Spock has sometimes been accused of fostering a climate of permissiveness, but that charge cannot be substantiated. He was, however, a symbol of a new approach to parenting. "It was the idea that one could devote oneself entirely to raising the children. Further, these children could become the brightest and healthiest and most assured ever."[3] The effect of Spock's work was to foster the development of a child-centered society.

The lessons that baby boomers were learning suggested they were the center of the world, and they could have anything they wanted. They came to believe that happiness could be found in the accumulation of things. It is not surprising that the 1970s became known as the "me" decade, and that baby boomers have been accused of selfishness and materialism. After all, other people helped to make them that way.

## National Optimism

The birth years of baby boomers coincided with a time of national optimism which lasted almost as long as the boom itself. That optimism arose in part because of unparalleled opportunities in the work place, in the vastness of consumer goods, and in the enjoyment of life. There was a feeling of inevitable progress. "The sky is the limit," and "You can be anything you want," typified the climate of the day.

In addition, optimism rose from America's place in the world. After the Second World War most Americans held strongly to the conviction that they were the greatest nation on earth. America had not only proved itself victorious and invincible, it was also recognized that America was good and morally upright. The United States of America was truly the land of opportunity where generosity, fairness, and tolerance were shown to all.

This engendered in baby boom children a sense of hope, both economically and politically, and created feelings of security and optimism for the future. When that bubble eventually burst, it contributed to disillusionment and cynicism.

## The Family Ideal

In the late 1940s, and particularly in the 1950s, the ideal of the family was deeply imbedded in American society. That cultural ideal gave rise to what Jones describes as the "procreation ethic" which flourished during the years of the baby boom. The procreation ethic was impressed on families deeply and constantly, like water dripping on a stone. It's rules were clear and unmistakable:  1) it was preferable to marry than not marry;  2) it was preferable to be a parent than a non-parent; 3) it was preferable not to have an "only" child." [4]

It was not simply that "family" was in style, but that it was portrayed as the key to happiness. The family was seen as essential for wholeness, and its emergence on center stage in the play of life-happiness was instilled in all the children who were part of the cast.

## *The Role of Television*

Baby boomers were the first generation to grow up in a world where television was a way of life. Most never knew their home without it. For many, it became the babysitter.  Paul Light, an authority on the baby boom, writes: "By the time the average baby boomer reached the age of sixteen, he or she had watched from 12,000 to 15,000 hours of TV," or the equivalent of 24 hours a day for 16 to 20 solid months. [5] Jones reports an even higher total: 24,000 hours, on average, by the time a baby boom child reached 18 years.[6]  Light points out the impact of all that viewing:

- It taught about adulthood without benefit of parent or teacher.
- It presented a world of remarkable similarity.
- It crowded out other sources of information.
- It fostered social separation.
- It reduced time spent in conversation and human interaction. [7]

In support of that last point, it is helpful to be aware of a study Jones cites which reveals "a forty year decline in the amount of time parents spend with their children, much of the recent loss due to television." [8]

What the baby boom saw on television portrayed a fantasy world, with a vision of the American family that was both unrealistic and unattainable. Children were watching programs like "Leave It To Beaver," "Ozzie and Harriet," and "Father Knows Best." They saw an idealized world which never encountered difficult problems or raised complex issues. It was a world of white middle-class families whose greatest difficulties could always be happily resolved within thirty minutes. It is not surprising that the baby boom generation has had so much trouble coming to grips with some of the uncomfortable realities of family life.

## The Impact of Advertising

A major part of the effect of television came from the thousands of commercials beamed at baby boom children, as many as 300,000 of which may have been seen by the time an average boomer reached the age of 21. These commercials were designed to create and stimulate desire. While that is always true of advertising, the baby boom "was the first generation of children to be isolated by Madison Avenue as an identifiable market. That is the appropriate word: *isolated*. Marketing, and especially television, *isolated* their needs and wants from those of their parents."[9] This

advertising strategy was highly successful.
Children could recite advertising jingles before
they could speak in sentences, and could
identify product brands long before they could
read. That the commercials did their job could
be proven in the cereal section of the
supermarket, where one could hear the shrill
demands of children for products that had been
effectively planted in their want zones.

With all this, baby boomers began to
develop economic power. They created fads
like coonskin caps, hula hoops, and Barbie
dolls. Television advertising not only increased
their desire for material things and contributed to the belief that "things" were the key to
happiness, it also taught them that their
generation had power.

*The Role of Education*

Education, we have suggested, was a
distressing experience for some baby boomers.
There were so many of them that they were
often dealt with in groups and treated as a
"generational unit." Paul Light says, "They
grew up as the first standardized generation,
drawn together by the history around them, the
intimacy of television, and the crowding that
came from the sheer onslaught of other baby
boomers."[10] One result was an emerging sense
of bondedness. They drew ideas from one
another, developed a strong reliance on peer
groups, and found an appreciation for the
common good of their generation.

There was another side to this, however. The crowding to which they were subject may have given rise to three traits commonly seen in 25 to 45-year-olds today, which are:

- a deep need for privacy;
- a lifelong commitment to individualism;
- a desire for physical space.

One aspect of their education — which may be virtually unknown to most older Americans — made a lasting mark on many baby boomers. I refer to the air-raid drills which became "a bizarre weekly drill none of them has forgotten. The baby boomers never forgot the lesson that their world could end in a flash of light and heat while they were crouched helplessly in gymnasiums and basements..."[11] Jones reminds us that the protestors at Three Mile Island in 1979 were the kids who had gone through air raid drills in the schools of the 1950s.

A deep-seated fear of nuclear war is one significant factor in the psychological development of the early boomers. Other shaping factors tended to make them idealistic, materialistic, optimistic, and bonded to one another.

## LATER SHAPING FACTORS

Perhaps nothing is more important for understanding the baby boom generation than to recognize how the traumatic events of the 1960s affected them. This is particularly true for those born before 1955. If the baby boomers' nostalgia for the 50s is a reflection of the desire to experience again the safety and security of their early childhood, perhaps the pre-occupation with the 1960s is evidence of the need to understand what happened in their later development.

Our society seems to enjoy going back to the 1960s. In recent years, dozens of books and magazines have focused on that decade. We still are not not sure what really happened then. Just running through the list is enough to make one wonder how vulnerable people withstood so many devastating blows.

## The Cold War

We have spoken of the trauma baby boomers experienced from the air-raid drills which were part of their educational experience. As the cold war developed and deepened, many baby boomers came to the conviction that the world would end in a nuclear nightmare. The Cuban missile crisis intensified that fear. Someone has suggested that for many boomers, the question was not if a nuclear holocaust would come, but when. In a book called *By the Bomb's Early Light,* author Paul Boyer argues that "nuclear fear was the shaping cultural force from the mid-1940s to the mid-1960s."[12] The seeds of fear planted in baby boomers' childhood bore fruit in their pessimism about the future which emerged in the 1960s.

This fear may help explain why baby boomers seem to have so little success in saving money, and why they live so much for the moment. Baby boomers grew up believing that they had to live for today. Events in recent history which have done so much to reduce the threat of war cannot compensate for the twenty or more years in which most of the baby boomers lived with the nightmare of, what seemed to them, the inevitability of nuclear war.

## *The Assassinations*

For first wave baby boomers, the most traumatic public event as they grew up was the assassination of John Kennedy. It hardly needs to be said that this tragic act stunned the nation, but its impact on the young was especially severe. Kennedy was known to them because of television, they identified with him because he was a father, and they responded to his warmth and humanity. They witnessed the shocking scenes of his death and its aftermath. It was the ultimate television event, and as Americans were glued to their TV sets during those terrible November days, the horror of the president's death continued to be felt. Years later, one young man talked about the impact of that death on his life. He said, "nothing bad had ever happened to me before. Suddenly I found myself in a world where nothing was safe." For many baby boomers Kennedy's death meant the loss of both security and innocence.

*The Vietnam War*

Probably nothing so crystalized and symbolized a generation as the reaction which most baby boomers had to the Vietnam War, which Jones describes as "a generational obsession." While they had nothing to do with the decision to wage that war, they were the ones who fought it. "The terrible price of Vietnam was paid by the entire country. But no one felt it more directly or more personally than the 26.8 million men of the baby boom who came of draft age between 1964 and 1973. In Vietnam, there were 58,000 killed and 153,000 wounded, the overwhelming majority of them baby boomers. The war created 35,000 widows and orphans."[13]

More than a million baby boomers saw combat in Vietnam. When the agonizing struggle came to an end, they returned to an America which could not deal with the war, and therefore ignored or rejected the veterans who returned home. As we all know, our society is still dealing with problems and needs which resulted.

The scars of that war are borne not only by those who fought it, but by millions of baby boomers who lived for eight years with the sword of the draft hanging over their heads. Nor was the effect felt only by men. While women were not subject to the draft, they also experienced the pain of that war. Women served in Vietnam too, and suffered there, and many nursed the wounds of other sufferers. Those whose boyfriends, husbands, brothers, and friends faced the trauma of the draft shared in the agonizing uncertainty of that experience, and waited and worried during tours of duty. Vietnam was devastating to millions. "The optimism and hope that the boom generation took into the Vietnam years only made its eventual disappointment more devastating. They had been young and idealistic and Vietnam made them old and cynical."[14]

The Vietnam war shattered for many the belief in both the moral superiority and the physical power of America. It destroyed faith in leadership and created a permanent distrust of institutions. As Paul Light points out, "Americans of all ages lost faith in their institutions and leaders in the 1960s, and have yet to recover." [15]

## Racial Unrest

Civil rights was one lesson learned well in the education of the baby boom; it connected with their sense of fairness and tolerance. The civil rights act of 1964 made integration a reality for many. Martin Luther King, Jr. was one of their heroes. By the time the freedom riders had gone south, the baby boom was largely committed to the principle of civil rights.

There was a down side to this hopeful climb. The vivid depictions of civil rights workers being harassed and abused stirred the baby boom generation to anger. Then came the assassination of Dr. King, with its aftermath of riots in the cities, including pictures on television of whole blocks on fire. Once again, it was apparent to them that America is not fair, and that liberty and justice for all is just another empty promise.

## The Breakup of the Family

In spite of the glorification of the ideal of family and all the focus on marriage in the 1950s, many of the baby boomers witnessed the breakup of their own parents' marriages. Writing in 1980, Landon Jones could say, "Each year since 1960, the total number of children affected by divorce in the United States, has gone up." [16] That initial surge in divorce rates was the result of the baby boomers' parents ending their marriages. Not only did that take its toll in terms of the trauma divorce always causes in children, but it was also one more breach of security, another experience of disappointment, another broken promise, another futile dream.

## The Economic Squeeze

Most baby boomers were raised to believe they could have it all. The promise was that education would provide a ticket to a guaranteed future, and it seemed to do so, at least for the first of them who moved quickly from college into the market place, and found the promise of their dreams coming to fulfillment. But for most of them, that did not happen. For all the hope and promise of affluence, most baby boomers have experienced economic hard times. This is particularly true of younger baby boomers.

Many baby boomers are finding it difficult to manage. On virtually every available economic indicator, the baby boom is lagging behind past generations. Paul Light reports that 20 percent of them are at or below the poverty level. That may be surprising, since we seem to hear mostly about the "yuppies" (a term many baby boomers resent). Stay with that word for just a moment. It means, of course, young urban professionals (or young upwardly mobile professionals) and refers to the upscale, affluent, trendy, young adults who are usually pictured driving Volvos and BMW's and enjoying life in the fast lane. It is important to recognize that not more than 5 percent of baby boomers are — or have been — "yuppies." For the majority, life has been economically hard. In terms of real dollars, most are losing ground.

Failure to achieve economic success and inability to satisfy the desire to acquire possessions frustrates one of the earliest and strongest of the baby boomers great expect-ations. That deep disappointment has given rise in many to frustration, resentment, and self-doubt. Certainly that is not true of all. Many of the baby boomers have done well, both economically and emotionally. Many remain hopeful. Yet for the overwhelming majority, early experiences in life seemed to promise more than life has delivered.

As we have sought to understand the development of baby boomers, we have identified shaping and reshaping factors. For the most part, early life experiences shaped in them great expectations. Optimism, the anticipation of material prosperity, hopefulness, fairness, and idealism were the milk on which they were raised. The traumatic events of the 1960s produced a great reversal. For many of them, adolescence and early adulthood produced a feeling of being unable to adjust to society, or the belief that society could not adjust to them. If, in looking at the baby boom generation, we see things we do not understand, or do not approve of, we do well to remember the up and down seesaw ride many of them experienced in their shaping years. Perhaps no other generation has had a higher "high" or fallen so unexpectedly to such a devastating "low." They are a group which entered adulthood staggered by change, shocked by tragedy, questioning all assumptions, and groping to find their way.

[1] Cheryl Russell, *100 Predictions For The Baby Boom.* New York: Plenum Press, 1987, p. 38.

[2] Landon Jones, *Great Expectations, America and the Baby Boom Generation.* New York: Bellantine Books, 1980, p. 53.

[3] *Ibid.,* p. 56.

[4] *Ibid.,* p. 31

[5] Paul Light, *Baby Boomers.* New York: W.W. Norton and Company, 1988, p. 123.

[6] Jones, Great Expectations. *America and the Baby Boom Generation.* p. 140.

[7] Light, *Baby Boomers.* p. 124.

[8] Jones, *Great Expectations, America and the Baby Boom Generation.* 139.

[9] *Ibid.,* p. 51.

[10] Light, *Baby Boomers.* p. 131.

[11] Jones, *Great Expectations, America and the Baby Boom Generation.* p. 59.

[12] Cited in Light, *Baby Boomers.* p. 139.

[13] Jones, *Great Expectations, America and the Baby Boom Generation.* p. 118.

[14] *Ibid.,* p. 119.

[15] Light, *Baby Boomers.* p. 159.

[16] Jones, *Great Expectations, America and the Baby Boom Generation.* p. 246.

# CHAPTER THREE

# The Baby Boom Today

During my childhood, I had a teacher who was fond of saying "You are what you are because you were what you were." The point she was making is that what we experience when we are young shapes our future. That remains generally true. In this chapter we will consider the factors which contributed to shaping of the baby boom generation — those born between 1946 and 1964 — and seek to identify some of the causes behind the patterns commonly seen in this group today.

Those who are older may throw up their hands in dismay over some of the attitudes and practices of this generation. It is helpful, however, to remember that our task is to *understand* people, not judge them. It should also be kept in mind that most of the factors which helped to make baby boomers what they are were quite beyond their control. Fault may be found for the weaknesses of any group, if that is what one is looking for. And yet, strengths and virtues may also be found in any group. Certainly, there are many of both in the baby boom generation.

As we examine these young adults, we will need to be aware of the warning of Landon Jones, who suggests that the baby boom is a moving target not easy to hit. It is diverse, made up of many different groups and types of people. It is unpredictable, constantly changing. Yet, there are common traits that fit vast numbers of people in this generational group, and we shall attempt to do that in order to increase our understanding and prepare us to minister to them.

## COMMON PATTERNS AND TENSIONS

*In Marriage and Family*

Students of the baby boom generation speak of the 3-D pattern:

- delayed marriage,
- deferred child-bearing, and
- divorced couples.

People in our society are marrying later than in previous generations. One result is a large number of singles in the 25 to 45 age group. As marriages are delayed, the probability increases of singles remaining single. When people do marry, they frequently postpone having children or even decide to have none at all. The birth rate keeps decreasing, and the result is smaller families. A recent report announced that household size in the United States had reached an all time low of 2.62 people, approximately half what it was a century ago, and it is expected to shrink further.

While the divorce rate is not increasing, it has stabilized at a very high rate. Cheryl Russell predicts that half of all baby boomers will divorce at least once, and in spite of greater longevity, only 13 percent of baby boom couples will celebrate a 50th wedding anniversary.[1]  When divorce does occur, re-marriage is becoming a less probable option.

With about half of all baby boom marriages ending in divorce, the majority of the baby boom's children will spend at least part of their childhood living with a single parent. Estimates are that about 10 percent of baby boomers will never marry. In fact, the baby boom is producing the largest group of 25 to 45-year-old singles the country has every known.

All of this, coupled with the baby boom's widely recognized acceptance of varied lifestyles, creates a diversity of living arrangements. Many people in this age group live together outside of marriage. In 1970, approximately 71 percent of American households consisted of married couple families. By 1989, that number had shrunk to 56 percent.

*Women in the Work Force*

A major and permanent change in American society has resulted from 25-45 year old women who are employed outside the home. Seventy percent are now working, and the number will reach 80 percent by 1995.[2] Not only are the vast majority of baby boom women working, but the majority of all mothers of young children are now employed. Roughly six out of ten mothers of children under the age of five are working outside the home.[3]

Three important consequences are evident from this pattern. First, many people are experiencing considerable stress. Women feel torn between work and family. Most of them need to work for economic reasons, but are struggling with conflicting emotions, as they are separated from their children. For the first time, perhaps, it is not just women who feel these stresses. They are new to baby boom men, as well. A second consequence is the great need for our society (including the church) to do more about child care. We are woefully short of nursery and day care facilities, and great concern is raised among these young parents about the quality of what now exists. This situation intensifies parental stress. A third consequence is that the church can no longer assume that activities can be planned for or carried out by women as in the past.

## The Pressure of Time

Some authorities insist that baby boomers have more free time than their parents did, but that is not a universal consensus. For example, baby boom author E. J. Kahn III cites a Louis Harris poll which indicates that, "Americans are working over five hours per week more than fifteen years ago, and have lost nearly ten hours of weekly leisure time."[4]

Certainly baby boomers believe they have less free time. For women, free time is all but squeezed out by the demands of work, home, and family. For baby boom men, part of what once would have been considered free time is now spent in sharing household and parenting tasks. While few would argue that fathers do as much as mothers in these areas, nearly everyone would agree that fathers today do more of these tasks than their fathers did. Cheryl Russell is bold enough to predict that "baby boom husbands will do one-third of the family housework . . ." [5]

The pressure of time is creating a tired generation. Kahn speaks at length about this tiredness. "We're so tired . . . Sure, our parents thought they were tired . . . but we are even more tired . . . A survey published in the *Journal of the American Medical Association* suggests that as many as one of every four of us has had a bout with chronic fatigue syndrome, which may or may not be a virus that may or may not be connected with depression." [6]

As far as a virus is concerned, "may not" is probably correct. According to a recent Reuters news release, depression, and not a virus, causes chronic fatigue syndrome, which is often called "yuppie flu."[7] While having "yuppie flu" might be deemed by some to be a status symbol, the loss of this explanation makes clear that chronic fatigue is not the result of a physical condition, but an emotional one. Chronic fatigue indicates that something is out of balance in one's life.

## Changing Values

While baby boomers share some of the same values as their parents and grand-parents, there are significant differences. The traditional values of marriage, family, home, and work are still of great importance to baby boomers. What makes them different is that each of these values lives in tension with an opposite and competing value. A push in one direction is met by a pull in another direction.

Take marriage as an example. Nine out of ten baby boomers affirm marriage as the best lifestyle. Most of them are married and hope to remain so — all quite traditional. Yet, their view of marriage is different than previous models, with two-thirds wanting their marriage to be a partnership in which husband and wife both work outside the home and share homemaking tasks.

The same tension exists in their view of family. Only 1 percent of baby boomers believe the childless couple is the ideal family. The majority believe that having two children is ideal. Ninety percent say their family is the most important thing in their lives. Most want more emphasis on traditional family ties. At the same time, they believe parents should pursue their own interests. "Few baby boomers have made any career sacrifices for their families," reports Cheryl Russell.[8] They believe in the primacy of the individual within the family. (An implication for those in the church is that it is no longer effective to appeal to the family as a group. This crucial point must be kept in mind as churches plan programmatic responses to the baby boom generation.)

A third value to consider is that of the home. The middle-aging of the baby boom is producing a trend for staying home. About 50 percent now stay home on Saturday night.

"Cocooning" and "couch potatoes" are the trendy terms to describe this phenomenon. Staying home exists in tension with the pull of the world. It appears that baby boomers are becoming more involved in their communities, and that they maintain interest in and concern about global issues. At home, or out? Many baby boomers want both.

A fourth area of tension is seen in the competing desires arising from seeking satisfaction in work and the desire for instant gratification. Most baby boomers have a high commitment to work. They believe work should be enjoyable, satisfying, and have value and meaning. At the same time, their life-long need for instant gratification means they do not want to work very long to achieve a goal. Here again is the push/pull pattern.

The values of the baby boom generation have changed far more radically than this section might imply. A major shift — with great consequence to the church — has occurred in American society, and is due in no small measure to this generation. The change is that "traditional concepts of right and wrong have been replaced by norms of 'harmful' or 'harmless'."[9] We are living in what has become an amoral world which seems to be either unable or unwilling to distinguish right from wrong.

Another indication of how radically values have changed in American society comes from *American Demographics* magazine.[10]

*Percentage of mothers who say the following traits are important to instill in their children:*

| Traits | Today | 1924 |
|---|---|---|
| Independence | 76% | 25% |
| Tolerance | 47% | 6% |
| Loyalty to church | 22% | 50% |
| Strict obedience | 17% | 45% |

This comparison illustrates what can only be seen as a drastic shift in values. Obedience, which was once considered important by nearly half of all mothers, is now felt to be necessary by less than one in five, while tolerance is given more than twice the importance of loyalty to church. Baby boomer values are significantly different than those of previous generations.

## Life Issues

While it might be possible to develop a more extensive list, at least three concerns impel the baby boomer. One is the search for self-fulfillment. Several years ago, Daniel Yankelovich wrote a fascinating book on this theme.[11] While the research on which his book is based is now somewhat dated, his basic points remain valid. Yankelovich argues that the search for self-fulfillment has become part of the fabric of American life, and reports that 80 percent of the American public identify with, and participate in, this quest to a greater or lesser degree.

Yankelovich points out that the search for self-fulfillment involves a great deal of introspection about one's inner needs and unfulfilled potentials. He argues that self-fulfillment is the opposite of self-denial (which is, of course, a basic ingredient in the call to Christian discipleship). One of the changes which has resulted in American society is that, "no moral virtue is attached any longer to the idea that it is good to curb the imperatives of the self."[12]

His key argument is that self-fulfillment cannot come through total freedom or by looking inward. "You are not the sum of your desires. You do not consist of an aggregate of needs, and your inner growth is not a matter of fulfilling all your potentials. By concentrating day and night on your feelings, potentials, needs, wants, and desires, and by learning to assert them more freely, you do not become a freer, more spontaneous, more creative self; you become a narrower, more self-centered, more isolated one. You do not grow, you shrink."[13]

In these remarkable words, Yankelovich provides an insight which helps us understand this widespread pattern in the baby boom generation (and in ourselves), and also paves the way for an approach of sensitively discussing this concern in conversations which may then provide opportunity for a positive lifting up of the good news of Jesus Christ.

A second issue which drives baby boomers is the search for meaning. Paul Light reports in baby boomers "a growing search for individual meaning."[14] Perhaps this is due in part to the normal concern about mortality as one ages, but surely it also arises because of the failure to find meaning in the places one has sought it.

Peter Hoffman, in a recent article in the *New York Times* titled "The 'Flee Decade" suggests that the 1970s were the "Me" decade, growing from the emphasis on getting more for oneself. He describes all that his generation has acquired, or at least those who have managed to find material prosperity. "We have become slaves to money, like the very people we once detested," he writes.

Money and the other symbols of "success" have not brought satisfaction. "All I hear these days is 'I've got to do something else.' Or, 'I've got to change my life.' Or, 'There's gotta be something better'." Hoffman goes on to say, "These are not the usual sighs after a tough day. These are the words of people in real self-doubt. If friends of mine in various fields are a barometer of what our thirty-something brothers and sisters are thinking, it appears that we've about reached the end of our respective ropes."[15]

Hoffman's title comes from his observation that many disillusioned baby boomers are "talking in deadly serious tones about giving it all up," and taking off somewhere. The key sentence in his piece is this: "I think we are trying, after all these years, to once again find ourselves."

He is surely correct in his diagnosis, even though the prescription he suggests is unlikely to provide a cure. Not very many will try that strong medicine, and few who do will be helped much by it. It is the diagnosis which deserves our attention.  Great numbers of people have found, as they approach mid-life, that the road they have been traveling is actually a treadmill.  They don't need to be convinced that they are not getting anywhere, they already know it.  Those who can point to another way, with sincerity and humility, have an audience.

Baby boomers are involved in a search for self-fulfillment and a search for meaning. They are also engaged in a search for safety and security.  This need has obvious roots in some of their life-shaping experiences, and can be found with consistency in the boomer generation.  Whether it is true for all is open to question, but millions share a concern about these issues, and an increasing number are attempting to do something about them.

One manifestation of the search for meaning is in concern for the environment. Environmentalism is anger about acid rain, oil spills, chemical pesticides, toxic waste.  It also concerns issues closer to home.  "It is about radon, asbestos, toxic-waste sites, undrinkable water, smog alerts, overflowing garbage dumps — and anger at the deteriorating quality of life in one's community."[16]  Baby boomers have brought this issue to the forefront of American consciousness.  Earth Day is primarily a baby boom phenomenon. Because of such concern, environmentalism "could well become the most universal and potent political theme of the 1990s."[17]  Concern about the environment is the baby boom generation's greatest social priority.

A second component in their search for safety has to do with fears of nuclear power.

Many remain deeply concerned about a growing reliance on that source of energy.

A third aspect of concern for safety is evident in the choices many are making in their personal lifestyles, particularly in matters of health, diet, and physical fitness. Baby boomers, for example, reduced their consumption of alcoholic beverages, leading to a 4.2% decline in distilled products sales in 1989.

These significant areas of the baby boomers' search for fulfillment provide points of contact, conversation, and cooperation for the church interested in ministry with that generation. As attention is given to their search, ideas about how a church may be in ministry with them will also begin to emerge.

## COMMON CHARACTERISTICS

We have attempted to provide a portrait of this generation by taking time to create a clear image which represents them fairly. Let us look briefly at a number of additional snapshots which provide further images of this unique generation.

### High expectations

We can now understand the significance of the title of Landon Jones' book, *Great Expectations*, which describes a fundamental characteristic of this age group. During their formative years, America was enjoying unparalleled material prosperity, making tremendous scientific and medical advances, and continually expanding the frontiers of knowledge. Boomers' high level of education also contributed to their "great expectations." An article on "Boomer Blues" in *Psychology Today* makes this observation: "Our soaring expectations went beyond consumer goods into nonmaterial matters. We came to expect our jobs to be more than a way to make a living. Work now needs to be ecologically innocent, comfortable to our dignity, a call to growth and excitement, a meaningful contribution to society — and deliver a large paycheck. Married partners once settled for duty, but today's mates expect to be ecstatic lovers, intellectual colleagues, and partners in tennis and water sports. We even expect our partners to be loving parents, a historical peculiarity to anyone versed in the Victorian child-rearing model."[18]

It hardly needs to be pointed out that these are unrealistic expectations. What does need to be recognized is that baby boomers are not emotionally prepared for unhappiness and the greater one's expectations, the higher the probability and degree of disappointment. In spite of many such disappointments, high expectations remain, and the potential for disillusionment continues.

### The Psychology of Affluence

Yankelovich describes this phenomenon which arose early in baby boomers' expectations. It involves the assumption that the continual accumulation of possessions is both possible and desirable. "Acquiring more of everything is a matter of personal entitlement rather than a mere hope or dream." In the psychology of affluence, "personal desire achieves the status of ethical norm."[19]

Changes in the economic world over the past two decades have forced baby boomers to come to terms with a world of limits. "Many baby boomers fear that the days of endless possibility are over." [20] Some have chosen to lower their expectations of having. It is no longer true that when you ask baby boomers what they want, they invariably say "more," as was the case when Yankelovich asked that question. The idea of a simplified lifestyle carries appeal for many people in the baby boom generation. Yet the deeply rooted psychology of affluence continues to be a factor in the lives of most.

## Emotional Expressiveness

Do you remember when a common slogan expressed by young people was, "Let it all hang out"? That sentiment from the boomers' youth continues to play a role — although in a more refined manner — in their generation today. They have been and are still eager to be in touch with and express feelings. They believe in giving free and open expression to one's emotions, sincerity and honesty in human interaction. They despise hypocrisy and respect genuineness.

## Individualism

Baby boomers have a strong commitment to individualism. Paul Light describes this pattern as he reports that boomers reject labels of any kind, they have little use for titles and prefer to use first names in all contexts, they have little brand loyalty, prefer not to identify with any political party; and are strongly committed to freedom of choice. All this is due to their strong bent toward individualism.

This commitment to individuality helps explain the high degree of tolerance and diversity among baby boom people. "The baby boom is united in its tolerance of diversity . . . accepting and even encouraging individual differences and alternate lifestyles. The result is an increasingly diverse culture . . ." [21] This diversity "is more than tolerance, it is a belief that what is right for me is right for me, and what is right for you is right for you. Even absolutes seem to be relative." [22]

## Distrust of Institutions

An enduring legacy of the 1960s is an anti-institutional bias on the part of the baby boom generation. "Americans of all ages lost faith in their institutions and leaders in the 1960s, and have yet to recover [that faith]," says Paul Light.[23] Yankelovich points out that "in our preoccupation with self-fulfillment, we have grown recklessly unrealistic in our demands on our institutions."[24] No doubt that is true, but the fact remains that those in the boom generation are still operating with an anti-institutional bias.

While all institutions suffer from that negative bias, the church is particularly hard hit. Light cites a 1985 Louis Harris poll which indicates that for baby boomers, organized religion represents one of the least trusted of all institutions, and boomers are the least trusting of all age groups. [25] Evidence of a continuing distrust can be seen in a number of ways, from the low level at which baby boomers participate in the life of a church, to their reluctance to join a congregation, to their lack of interest in identifying with a denominational body, and to the ease with which they depart from a congregation.

Leith Anderson makes a helpful comment on the "departure" issue by pointing out that baby boom church goers today see a congregation as a "way station." "One church is chosen and joined for one chapter of life, but there is great ease in moving along to the next church (at the next 'way station') when the next chapter begins." As Anderson notes further, this is "a particularly confusing and painful experience to the pastor who comes from an older generation and sees such mobility as a church rejection if not a personal rejection." [26]

We have noted that many baby boomers have an inclination toward non-affiliation. Part of this stems from their difficulty in making a commitment, and part from institutional distrust. Over the past few years, there has been a considerable increase in the number of people (especially young adults) who attend a church, but do not join. In all likelihood, this trend will continue.

Another aspect of institutional distrust is baby boomers' apparent disinclination to affiliate with a denominational group. Several factors lie behind this attitude, including this age group's mobility, a growing concern for interest and control to be exercised locally, and a lack of denominational loyalty. A key consequence is that very few churches will have guaranteed constituencies, and congregations need to work intentionally to gain and keep new members.

In addition to the characteristics we have looked at, many others could be added. Here are some general observations. Baby boomers tend not to be guilt motivated, and do not respond to "shoulds" and "should-nots." They value self-reliance, and have a strong independent streak. They are introspective, and considerably given to self-analysis. Paul Light speaks of the legacy of the 1960s producing a sense of wistfulness and unfulfilled dreams. Baby boomers are pragmatic, with a strong interest in what works. They rely on their own experience. And, they are given to questioning. More than any other generation, baby boomers are inclined to compare, question, and analyze.

To conclude this chapter, consider this short list of various lifestyle ingredients which are increasingly evident in the lives of baby boomers, and those which seem to be decreasing. You can see many of the underlying influences we have already discussed, and how they are manifested in specific ways.

## *Increasing*

Weekend getaways
VCRs
Sunday as family time
Take out food
Golf
Shopping at home
Saving money
Gardening

Reading books
Home-ownership
Nostalgia
Ethnic restaurants
"Genuine" toys (Lincoln
    Logs &Erector Sets)
Choosing parenthood
Four wheel drive vehicles

## *Diminishing*

Housewives
Meal time as family
Two week vacations
Wanting more choices
Reading newspapers
High heels
High cholesterol foods
Household projects
Conforming (as always)

Singles hangouts
Attending live arts
    performances
Relocating
Planning for early
    retirement
Living in the suburbs (only
    12% do)
Skiing

[1] Cheryl Russell, *100 Predictions For The Baby Boom.* New York: Plenum Press, 1987., p. 18.

[2] *Ibid.,* p. 19.

[3] *1990 Almanac of Consumer Markets.* American Demographics Press.

[4] *The Boston Globe*, 1988. Reprinted in *REVIEW*, January 1989, p. 22. The same poll is cited in Cheryl Russell, *100 Predictions for the Baby Boom.* p. 137. Russell reports the figure as eight hours less free time each week.

[5] Russell, *100 Predictions for the Baby Boom.* p. 18.

[6] *The Boston Globe, op. cit.*

[7] *Chicago Tribune*, July 4, 1990.

[8] Cheryl Russell, "The Sure Thing," *American Demographics Magazine*, August, 1988. The material in this section is based on this article.

[9] Daniel Yankelovich, *New Rules.* New York: Random House, 1981 p. 88.

[10] *American Demographics.* December, 1988, p. 10.

[11] Daniel Yankelovich, *New Rules* (New York: Random House, 1981) p. 88.

[12] *Ibid.,* pp. 88, 78.

[13] *Ibid.,* p. 242.

[14] Light, *Baby Boomers.* p. 245.

[15] *New York Times*, February 8, 1990.

[16] *Business Week*, September 25, 1989, p. 154.

[17] *Ibid.*

[18] *Psychology Today*, October, 1988.

[19] Yankelovich, *New Rults.* pp. 188, 189.

[20] Russell, *100 Predictions*, p. 47.

[21] *Ibid.,* p. 45.

[22] Leith Anderson. *Dying for Change.* (Minneapolis: Bethany House Publishers, 1990), p. 64.

[23] Light, *Baby Boomers.* p. 159.

[24] Yankelovich, *New Rults.* p. 5.

[25] Light, *Baby Boomers.* p. 160.

[26] Leith Anderson. *Dying for Change.* p. 20.

# CHAPTER FOUR

# Common Felt Needs Among Baby Boomers

For this book, I have chosen to separate three primary "areas of need" from the list of issues and concerns of the baby boom generation. I do so for two reasons. First, because a case can be made that the needs which will be discussed here are, in fact, the issues of greatest concern and significance to this generation. Second, because they are the needs to which the church can respond and, through responding, provide the greatest likelihood of connecting. By "connecting," I mean not simply gaining a hearing, but making a difference. These are the hungers for which the church can provide bread.

## A Longing for Spiritual Reality

Anyone who spends time listening to baby boomers will probably hear evidence of dissatisfaction, perhaps even of emptiness. "Wistfulness" is the term Paul Light has used to describe this pattern. The word means "characterized by unfulfilled longing or desire". It conveys a sense of pathos, a feeling of sorrow that what one has longed for may not be found. We have noted earlier that the "great expectations" of the baby boomers make them particularly vulnerable to disappointment.

However, here we focus, not so much on unfulfilled dreams, as on unfulfilled lives.

It is not difficult to document the sense of a basic lack, an empty core, in the lives of many baby boomers. One can see it all around in our culture, including in books and films. That emptiness, of course, is not unique to baby boomers. It has been present since people were old enough to understand their feelings. What is more recent is the recognition that what is longed for has not been found where people have been looking, and that the search has been going on long enough to show it isn't fruitful. For all their celebration of freedom and pursuit of material gain, the baby boom generation has awakened to the fact that they have come up empty. What is significant is that this is being recognized and acknowledged, especially by those who have managed to carve out the largest slice of the pie.

*American Demographics* magazine recently featured an article on the New Age movement. A major focus of the article was an emphasis on the type of people who are responding to New Age thinking. "Affluent baby boomers are the group most likely to embrace the so-called New Age movement." In analyzing the appeal to "educated, affluent, successful people," the author came up with this reason: "They are hungry for something that mainstream society has not given them. They say they are looking for 'alternatives,' 'new paradigms,' 'social transformation,' 'personal wholeness,' 'enlightenment,' and even 'utopia'." [1]

The article goes on to cite a survey which estimates that the New Age movement has approximately *11.5 million serious adherents*, and with the recent popularizing of the movement "... that figure is probably a good deal larger." I can hardly imagine those figures are accurate. Still, we may well be awed by the massive "success" of the New Age movement.

Now the reasons for New Age success. We have quoted the explanation given by the author, which suggests that it is primarily a sense of inner emptiness, a wistful longing, or a spiritual quest that has led people into New Age. One person quoted in the article was more specific, pointing out that those in the New Age movement "... don't care for existing religions, so they have come out with a new kind of religion — a New Age one, a kind of attunement."

We do well to give attention to what this person is saying, and not underestimate the fervor with which "existing religions" are being rejected. It will not be easy to surmount this attitude. Institutions do not change readily, and the church is no exception. Major changes will be required in congregations if they are to have an effective ministry with the baby boom generation.

It intrigues me that this article in such a "cutting edge" magazine places such stress on the *status* of the New Age clientele. In this short article, I counted twenty-four references to their social standing: affluent - 4, high income - 5, highly educated - 6, successful - 2, professional - 2, discriminating - 2, world-travellers - 1, creative - 1, and trend-setters - 1.

Obviously, someone is eager to point out that the followers of New Age are the elite, the cream of the crop.

The point to which I return is that if anyone could find fulfillment in what the world has to offer, these people should be expected to have found it. All the commonly accepted avenues to fulfillment were open to them: education, money, travel, success, status. Yet, they are still searching.

In its closing paragraph, the article raises a question about the future of New Age. "It's possible that the recent boom in New Age interest will turn out to be a fad fueled by bored, restless baby boomers." The author discounts that possibility. None of us has any idea how long the New Age movement will be popular. What we do know is that the basic spiritual hunger which has led many people into New Age will continue as long as people persist in looking for fulfillment where it cannot be found.

The spiritual hunger of the baby boom is identified by other observers. John Naisbitt, in *Megatrends 2000,* suggests that America is probably on the verge of a major religious awakening or revival.[2] In 1985, Craig Dykstra, then at Princeton Theological Seminary, wrote a thought-provoking editorial in *Theology Today*, in which he raises the possibility that we may be on the threshold of a religious awakening.[3] Dykstra quotes John Wheeler, introduced as president of the Center for the Vietnam Generation, who says: "Questions of faith and spirit have emerged strongly at the close of this decade [especially] among that cohort of the population we call the baby boomers." Wheeler gives three reasons: First, the baby boom generation has faced and remembers death. Second, this is a time of re-evaluation for many, a time of asking what all the striving and acquiring finally amount to, and what really does have value. Wheeler points out that material security and self-concern do not save us from a sense of spiritual void. Third, Wheeler mentions science, "which, though it gives us no final answers, drives us to metaphors reminiscent of Genesis."

Against this background, Dykstra raises questions about how the church will respond to this longing for spiritual fulfillment that is going on around it. He suggests that those who approach the church in their search will probably do so with some hesitation. In light of the common baby boom attitude of distrust for religious institutions, Dykstra is surely right. He is also right, I believe, in identifying that which those who do approach the church are truly seeking: "The deepest question they are asking — and may not yet dare to ask out loud — is this: Do you know God? If they sense we do not, again they will go away — perhaps this time more sadly than cynically. And if they sense we do, it will not be because we *say* we do. It will be because they see it in the way we live, in the manner of our speaking, and in our willingness to listen and to search. They will see it in the freedom this knowledge provides, and in what this knowledge commits us to."

Yes. If there is one thing the world has a right to expect of the church, it is the

knowledge of God. That God can be known
because God has made himself known, that we
know him because he has found us, and that
we will open our lives and our churches so that
others who hunger for God may be satisfied.
That is what we want to help baby boom
pilgrims understand and believe.

## A Hunger for Community

This is the second great need evident in
the baby boom, and again it is one to which the
church is surely able to respond. The hunger
for community is frequently identified as an
important concern of this generation. Daniel
Yankelovich speaks of this at some length. "A
hunger for deeper personal relationships
shows up in our research findings as a
growing concern . . . [Our] surveys show that
70 percent of Americans now recognize that
while they have many acquaintances they have
few close friends — and they experience this as
a serious void in their lives."[4]

The absence of community not only
produces loneliness, which is a common
enough problem, but also gives rise to deeper
distress. The absence of community, says
Yankelovich, "is experienced as an aching
loss, a void, a sense of homelessness. The
symptoms of its absence are feelings of
isolation, falseness, instability, and
impoverishment of spirit."[5]

But what is community? Yankelovich
points out that while it is not easy to define the
term, it can be understood by the feelings it
evokes, such as: "Here is where I belong, these

are my people, I care for them, they care for me, I am part of them, I know what they expect from me and I from them, they share my concerns, I know this place, I am on familiar ground, I am at home."[6]

The United Methodist Church held a conference on the theme "Reaching for the Baby Boomer." One of the features was a panel made up of baby boomers. Someone asked one of the women a question about what community meant to her. This is what she said: "Community is being there for each other when we have a need, or are needed. Relationships are very important to me, and must be characterized by loyalty and commitment. I value acceptance of me as I am, the honesty which lets me be myself, the feeling that we can disagree without harming the relationship. That is community."

We live in a society in which that kind of community is hard to come by. Many baby boomers struggle with commitment. In their busy lives, relationships tend to be formed primarily in the workplace, and time and circumstances make it difficult for such relationships to move beyond superficiality. Community is dependent on an ongoing and time-consuming process, and many people are too busy to engage in it.

Beyond reasons of time lies a deeper problem — our struggle for intimacy. Often that word is used in a sexual context, but of course it is much broader and richer than that. Intimacy has to do with relationships which are close, lasting, and personal, in which people are known to one another as they truly are, and relate in genuineness and depth.

An article on intimacy appeared recently in the *Chicago Tribune*. The author points out that "when we talk about intimacy, we're talking about being able to share our inmost self with someone else, and having that sharing reciprocated." While that is what many people would like, most do not know how — or where — to find it. The article quotes a professor of psychology who has written a book on intimacy: "Today, intimacy is harder for us, so we're more preoccupied with it. What I hear is a feeling of resignation. People realize they're not finding the fulfillment they had hoped to find." [7]

Robert Gribbon has done extensive research on baby boomers and their relationship with the church. His research points out that the desire for intimacy is a prime factor in bringing baby boomers back to church. "Those seeking the church are working primarily on the life issue of intimacy."[8] In his interviews with returnees, Gribbon noted "the overwhelming emphasis on belonging," and indicated that those turning to the church are looking for "friends, for a community of shared value, for support with life tasks, and a personalized but structured relationship with ultimate reality." [9]

Here then, is a need which the church is uniquely suited to address. The message of our faith is of a God who absolutely and unconditionally accepts us, and whose challenge to the faith community is, "As I have loved you, you also should love one another" John 13:34. At its best, the church is the home and family for which people are searching. True community can be found here and it exists, not just for those who now experience it, but for all whose hearts hunger for home.

## A Desire for Support with Life Tasks

Gribbon's research identified the desire to obtain support for life tasks as another important factor leading people in the baby boom generation to turn to the church.

Many baby boomers live apart from an immediate or extended family. Even where distance is not a factor, changes in lifestyles have weakened relationships with other relatives, and the amount of time spent with them is considerably less than it was in earlier eras. As a result, many feel they have no one to share in their struggle with life tasks.

Cheryl Russell identifies four primary life tasks in the lives of baby boomers: home, marriage, family, and work. She predicts that home and family concerns will dominate in the foreseeable future. "Because of the middle-aging of the baby boom, the United States is about to become a nation of homebodies... For the next two decades, the home will be the focus of American life, like it was in the 1950s."[10]   Family themes will be high on the agenda.

In another study, Robert Gribbon looked at people in their thirties, and explored issues to which the church could respond. Gribbon found that the day-to-day tasks of managing, parenting, and householding were a major concern for them. "Dissatisfaction with one's income, marriage, and parents tends to be greatest in the thirties," he noted.[11] This may give rise to a search for self-improvement.

While not the primary reason people seek the church, it is a factor. It has long been true that the arrival and rearing of children leads people to think about imparting values and providing religious training for children. One of the people Gribbon interviewed said, "I came for the sake of the children, but I found something for myself." Gribbon cites Hoge's study of Roman Catholic converts, which found "the religious instruction of children was a motivating factor for 45 percent of those who sought the church."[12] Gribbon takes pains to point out that people "may come to church for the sake of the children, but they don't stay for the sake of the children."

It is often a personal need for support which both attracts and involves people in the church. Life is complicated, and the need for encouragement and support is being increasingly recognized. A participant in a baby boom panel expressed the view of many when she indicated that she goes to church to find help in coping with the pressures of the week. "I go to church on Sunday," she said, "to find strength to get to Friday."

Specific ways in which the church can respond to needs like this will be dealt with later. For now, we simply point out that this area of need is also a prime area of concern to the church, and one in which the church has the capacity to make a significant contribution.

## THE LEGACY OF THE BABY BOOM

"The Legacy of the Baby Boom" is the title of the concluding chapter in Landon Jones' classic work, *Great Expectations*. As we complete our overview of this fascinating group of Americans, we will let Jones guide us in a brief look at some elements in the baby boom which are likely to endure:

- This is a generation that has always seen itself as unique, and can be understood as a generational unit.

- This is a generation that was once united in its conviction that it has a mission to develop fulfillment and harmony and to create wholeness in people.  Now it is moving from optimism to pessimism.

- This is a generation which grew up with unrealistic and unachievable expectations.  Now it has bumped up against limits.  "They had expected to be the masters of change, but now change has mastered them."[13]

- This is a generation that has helped create skepticism which challenges all our institutions and values.  Now authority is everywhere in decline, and all truth is relative.

- This is a generation that has redefined the family norm and allowed for the acceptance of a host of different lifestyles.

For better or worse, the baby boomers have changed American society; in many ways permanently. They have brought new freedoms, created new opportunities for women, raised the level of concern for the environment, contributed to the cause of world peace, reduced discrimination, lifted standards of excellence, stressed education, and made us more tolerant. They have also helped make our society more materialistic and self-centered, more skeptical and fragmented.

For all the changes they have created in society, they have had far less success in changing themselves. That is both a reason for disappointment and a source of hope. After all, they are still searching.

1 "The Aging of Aquarius," *American Demographics*. September, 1988, p. 34

2 John Naisbitt. *Megatrends 2000*. (New York: William Morrow & Co. 1990). p. 271.

3 *Theology Today*. July, 1985, p. 125.

4 Yankelovich, *New Rules*. p. 251.

5 *Ibid.*, p. 227.

6 *Ibid.*

7 Barbara Sullivan. "Close Encounters." *Chicago Tribune*, April 11, 1990.

8 Robert T. Gribbon, *When People Seek the Church*. Washington: Alban Institute Research Report. p. 17.

9 *Ibid.*, p. 18.

10 Cheryl Russell, "What's Going to Happen When the Baby Boom Gets Older?" *American Demographics Occasional Paper*, 1987.

11 Robert T. Gribbon. *Thirty Year Olds and the Church*. (Washington: Alban Institute Research Report, 1981). p. 9.

12 *Ibid.*, p. 12.

13 Landon Y. Jones. *Great Expectations: America and the Baby Boom* (New York: Random House, 1980). p. 389.

# CHAPTER FIVE

# Prerequisites to Reaching the Baby Boom

By this time, you may have read more about baby boomers than you ever thought you wanted to know. But understanding people is the necessary first step in being able to minister among them. I do admit to being somewhat weary with the term "baby boomer" myself, and many of those who are in that category don't care much for it either. I have chosen to use it because it has become so widely recognized, and it certainly fits better than "young adults." Not only is that phrase inaccurate and imprecise, the people we are talking about are characterized, not simply by their age, but by the attitudes and patterns they have in common. In any case, the term is apparently here to stay, and so we seem to be stuck with it.

Now, however, we must turn our attention to the church, and begin looking at what a congregation needs to be and do if it hopes to reach substantial numbers of this fascinating and complex group. What kind of church is going to be able to reach them? In my observations, the answer to that question is not found in external characteristics. While it can be documented that baby boomers who have joined churches seem to have shown a preference for larger congregations and for

independent churches, I believe that those
characteristics of churches are not so much
reasons for their choice as by-products of what
those churches provide and how they function.

It is important for us to consider why
certain churches seem preferred in order that
any church, no matter what its size, polity, or
affiliation, can attempt to carry out its ministry
in such a way as to be attractive to the baby
boom generation. Our study must begin by
looking at the internal life of the local church,
and the prerequisites necessary for a church to
be effective.

Prerequisite #1: *The Church Recognizes the*
*Need to Evangelize*

A problem which exists in many
congregations is a lack of interest in, and
sometimes even an aversion to, active
evangelism. Some reasons for that can be
readily identified. The introduction to this
volume spoke about people's discomfort with
evangelism, and suggested some explanations
for it. That discomfort is only one reason
evangelization is non-existent in many
churches. I believe at least three additional
causes can be identified.

First, there are some people in the
church who do not want the church to grow.
Occasionally that is openly stated, as when
someone says, "I like our church just the way
it is." Such a person might comment on the
desirability of knowing everyone and enjoying
close fellowship. More commonly, those who
do not want the church to grow will remain

silent about their feelings, but will resist new overtures in outreach or growth by objecting to any plan presented. Whatever the arguments they use, a probability is that they oppose growth because of the inconvenience it may bring, or the price they think they will have to pay. An unwillingness to make such a sacrifice leads such people to stand in the way of evangelization.

A second cause for the dearth of evangelization in many churches comes from those who do not think it is necessary. Included in this group are people who believe the church will grow automatically. Some have an attitude which suggests: "People know where we are and when we meet. If they want to come, they will." Those who think evangelism is unnecessary may say, "We don't need a special outreach strategy. If we just do our tasks well, the church will grow."

As I try to analyze what lies behind such statements, I see two different kinds of people, one whom I will call the "Older Leader," and the other the "Progressive Thinker." The Older Leader became active in the church after returning from service in the Second World War. For twenty years, he watched the membership of the church steadily increase with no evangelism committee, no outreach strategy, and only a single pastor staff. He does not see the need for an intentional effort in evangelism today. Consequently, he may remind people of the way things used to be, in the good old days, and if we only could have "the same old ------" things would be better.

The Progressive Thinker happens to be a baby boomer. While she also thinks active evangelization is unnecessary, her reasons are different. She believes it is inappropriate. The Progressive Thinker is a strong proponent of the tolerance which is a hallmark of her generation. She thinks everyone should be free to make their own choices independently, and is quite in sympathy — at least in this particular case — with the Older Leader's view that doing church tasks well is all that is necessary. She is uncomfortable with the idea of active evangelization. Her view of evangelism may be summed up as, "when new people show up we will be nice to them."

A third cause for churches' non-involvement comes from those persons who do not so much oppose evangelization as ignore it. They intellectually believe that evangelism is a Christian duty, but they either try to forget that fact, or rationalize a reason why it is not for them. Some of the people in this group — perhaps most — can easily be made to feel guilty about their lack of involvement. They have heard many times that all Christians are to be witnesses. The study of Scripture has persuaded them that this is true. However, their life experiences have convinced them that in their case it is not possible. They feel guilty about this, but not so much so that they are compelled to do something about it. When the subject of evangelism comes up, they let their silence speak for them.

Some of these people have made attempts along the way. A few of them have actually tried to talk about their faith with someone outside the church. In conversation they may have once murmured a few words about God, but after a pause they did not know what to say next and were relieved when the chance came to change the subject.

Others did, at one time, actually participate in an evangelism activity. The pastor made an appeal to them to take part in a community calling effort. They agreed out of a sense of duty and desire to support the pastor. They were somewhat surprised to discover how few other members showed up for this activity, but having come this far, they felt they could not very well back out, so they stayed. They were assigned a certain area to canvass. The plan was to identify the unchurched people who lived in that area so they could be followed up by the evangelism committee. (Thank God they hadn't been asked to serve on that!) The calls were completed, and no one slammed a door in their faces. The fact is, there were only two people in their area who did not claim to have a church, and neither of them seemed particularly eager to find one. The callers gave those names to the committee with no idea what was subsequently done with them. They remained quiet when the group leader talked about meeting again, and do not know whether the calling program continued.

The people who fall into this category fit the old cliche "once burned, twice shy." A distasteful experience in evangelization has confirmed their conviction that this work is not for them. Others in the church were so certain of that all along that they never even attempted an evangelizing task, and are not about to.

The fact that many of our churches are filled with the kind of people we have described must be recognized and dealt with before any evangelizing effort is to prove successful (to baby boomers, or anyone else). Let us imagine that a congregation's leaders go off on a planning retreat and come up with the idea of developing a blueprint for an evangelization plan for the congregation. They return and enthusiastically present the plan, only to be greeted with reactions ranging from indifference to opposition. The best response to their plan seems to be an attitude which says, "If that's what you want to do, go ahead." That response is not good enough; it's not even close. Plans need more than people's permission if they are to be successful.

Where, then, do we start? We must begin by helping the congregation recognize the need to be an evangelizing community.

An important point needs to be made here. Nearly all congregations have people within their ranks who would be glad to see the church add new members. After all, new members will contribute to the budget, as well as take on some ministry tasks now falling on the shoulders of the overburdened few. It is relatively easy to enlist people interested in membership recruitment as allies in a plan for evangelization. Since it seems so necessary to get support for such a plan, church leaders may be glad to accept those people with their reasons unchallenged. *It is a mistake to do so.* No plan for evangelization is likely to prove lastingly effective if it is based on a desire to simply get new members for the sake of easing a crunch in the church. We need to resist the temptation to take what seems to be a short-cut, and instead start down the longer road that goes in the right direction. What is in fact self-seeking is unlikely to be honored by God.

*Christian Century* magazine devoted attention to the subject of membership decline in mainline churches. One article suggested that a key reason was a loss of 'the evangelizing impulse'. The author declared that sometime around the middle of the century many churches "turned relativist, super tolerant, non-missionary." They "had been so used to retaining their children's loyalty and attracting their neighbors almost automatically, that they never learned the mandate of modernity: you have to be aggressive to hold your own and win the new."[1]

"Aggressive" is one of those words which makes people uncomfortable, especially when used in the context of evangelism. "Aggressive" is defined as "marked by driving forceful energy or initiative." The word contains two ideas that are very important when we think about evangelization. They are: "initiating" and "energetic."

"Initiating" makes us realize that "passive evangelism" is an oxymoron — a contradiction in terms. Evangelism is doing and telling, it is going and making disciples. Evangelism is action, and therefore always active, never merely waiting. Further, churches will simply not reach new people in any appreciable numbers if they rely on passive means of growth. Certainly, they will not reach unchurched people by waiting for them

to appear.  If there is one lesson the past
twenty-five years has taught, it is that
churches which ignore evangelism almost
certainly decline.   With the widespread
avoidance of evangelism in America's
churches, it is not surprising that 85 percent
are reported to be plateaued or declining.

"Energetic" is the other key idea in the
word "aggressive."  As applied to evangelism,
it calls for an enthusiastic embracing of the
task, and a strong effort in carrying it out.
That is the need; now look at how it may be
addressed.

Prerequisite #2:  *The Church Captures and
Communicates a Vision*

"Where there is no vision, the people
perish" says the King James Version  of
Proverbs 29:18.  That is certainly a provocative
idea.  Apply it to evangelization.  "Where there
is no vision" (for evangelism), "the people
perish" ("having no hope and without God in
the world," Ephesians 2:12).  The first step
toward reaching the baby boom, or any group,
is the development and communication of a
vision of the church as an evangelizing
community.

The vision for evangelization is God's.
God is its originator and source, and vision can
only come from God.  It needs to be caught.

Vision for evangelization is caught by
those whose lives have been transformed
through their relationship with God in Jesus
Christ, and who live in the joy and wonder of
the gift of God's transforming grace.  It is

experienced through their ongoing relationship with God, whose reality and empowering presence is continually enjoyed in worship and prayer as well as in the service performed in works on behalf of God's kingdom.

This evangelizing vision is beautifully illustrated in the life of the Apostle Paul, who not only anticipated with great longing the day when every knee would bow, and every tongue confess Jesus Christ as Lord (Phil. 2:10,11), but who so desperately longed for the vision's fulfillment that he could wish himself cut off from Christ if his people Israel could be saved (Romans 9:2).

That vision is the result of prayer, the prayer which leads one to know God, and in knowing God, to become like him. We become like God in the sense of having a heart like God's own heart, which aches for the children wandering aimlessly in the world, and whose love and compassion will not rest until they have come home.

Herb Miller suggests that "prayer opens the door that lets the mind of God into our thinking and behavior."[2] It is through prayer — personal and corporate — that the congregation will come to share God's vision of the church as an evangelizing community, and will experience that vision directing its thinking and behavior.

The vision is born in the pastor's own life of prayer and it is in the pastor's life that it must become incarnate. Unless the pastor is personally committed to the vision and is its chief communicator, in all probability the church will not be an evangelizing community.

One of the most important roles the pastor can fulfill is to be a visionary leader. God has chosen to use the ministry of human beings, placed in key leadership roles, to call and equip people for ministry (Ephesians 4:11,12). Unless the pastor of the church is the primary proponent of the church's vision and its chief communicator, the congregation will, in all likelihood, remain immobilized and the task of evangelization will continue to be ignored.

This is not to imply that visionary leadership is the task of one person. The pastor's role is unique and essential, but if the pastor is the only one advocating for the vision it will probably not permeate the congregation. The pastor needs allies.

Win Arn has suggested in his helpful *Church Growth Ratio Book* that a church can be transformed if the change being advocated is supported and encouraged by at least 60 percent of the official board, and at least 20 percent of the active members.[3] How can this happen? It begins as the pastor articulates the vision of the church as an evangelizing community before the members of the congregation's governing board.

Ideally, this task should begin at a leadership training retreat or similar occasion when the board members have time to reflect and pray, and do not have the pressure of an agenda. In communicating the vision, the pastor will emphasize the conviction that this is what the pastor believes God is calling both pastor and congregation to be and do. The pastor may speak of specific actions or changes that are taking place in the pastor's own life as a result of this call of God. The pastor may lead a study of Scripture passages which carry the evangelizing vision as the group spends time in prayer on this matter. Perhaps the pastor will suggest that if there are others who are hearing the call of God in this area that they inform the pastor.

It may be expected that there will be some response to this invitation. If not, the invitation may be repeated later. The pastor will invite those who respond to join together in a weekly time of prayer. Those prayer sessions will lift up the needs of the world, and focus on preparing the church to be an evangelizing community.

At the first board meeting following the retreat, an announcement about the prayer group may be made, and an invitation extended to others who wish to join. Each time the board meets, some time is given to the evangelizing vision. In the *Growth Report,* Win Arn suggests that one-third of each business meeting be spent focusing on issues of congregational growth and outreach.[4] Certainly this should include Bible study and prayer. The pastor and others may speak of how God is challenging them to evangelization and of ways in which they are personally responding. No one in the group should be manipulated or pressured into making a statement or taking action. Nothing is presented for a vote. However, invitations to join in the prayer sessions are given at each meeting of the board.

After a few weeks or months, the pastor will begin to engage the congregation in this process. They will be informed of what has been happening in the life of the pastor, the board, and the prayer group. An invitation may be given to anyone in the church family who shares or seeks the evangelizing vision to participate in the prayer group. The pastor will begin to consistently communicate certain themes to the congregation. These themes are dealt with in preaching, teaching, printed materials (bulletin and newsletter), and in conversations. They are not by any means the only themes addressed, and are not dealt with each week. They are, however, heard consistently.

The primary themes which are lifted up are these:

- People in our community have deep needs that Jesus Christ can meet.
- Life in the community of faith is a rewarding and fulfilling life.
- God wants to use our congregation to reach people who live apart from the church.
- This church can be an evangelizing community.

The messages should communicate hope and expectancy. They are intended to affirm the congregation and help people both to believe in the potential for evangelization and to be excited about the possibilities. They set forth a challenge and reminder that the church must "put as much effort into making disciples as we do into serving disciples." [5]

So the vision is communicated with clarity, consistency, and conviction. As it is, other voices in the congregation are also heard acknowledging and advocating it. A dream is born.

Prerequisite #3:  *The Church Has a Ministry Plan*

It may be assumed that all churches have essentially the same purpose, although not all would express it in the same way. Broadly speaking, the purpose of the church is to glorify and serve God.  We may further assume that all churches carry out essentially the same tasks.  While there may be considerably more variety in the description of those tasks, probably they could all be summarized in four broad categories: worship, nurture, fellowship, and mission. These are the four pillars which form the foundation on which the church stands.  All need to be strong if the church is to be effective.

In addition to recognizing and evaluating the faithfulness of the congregation in the universal tasks of ministry, a church needs to devote attention to its specific ministry at this time and in this place.  That calls for the development of what has been called a "philosophy of ministry" or a "statement of purpose," but may perhaps better be called a "ministry plan."

A ministry plan is a specific response to two questions:  Who are we trying to reach? and, How do we intend to reach them?  This book advocates that the "who" can be the baby boom generation, although that answer is too broad to be useful in a ministry plan.  Better answers would be "unchurched parents of pre-schoolers" or "single adults under thirty-five." The "how" question will necessitate the development of a plan which includes decisions about the styles to be adopted, the strategies to be employed, and the programs to be offered.

Developing a ministry plan involves two steps: learning and writing. Best results will be obtained if this responsibility is assigned to a task force made up of five to seven people. A task force is a group called together to deal with a single issue, continuing to function until the task has been completed. In my opinion the church's pastor must be a member of this task force, although not its chairperson. The chairperson ought to be someone who is to help everyone participate in the deliberation and keep the group on track. Members of the task force should all be enthusiastic advocates of the church as an evangelizing community. Both new and long-time members should be included, both men and women, and both younger and older members.

The task force's work begins with study. An early topic for discussion may well be a definition of the congregation's ministry area. Many people assume that the normal pattern is for each congregation to serve its own geographical neighborhood. (This is where the term "parish" originally came from.) While it is neither wise nor right for a church to ignore its community, the old concept of a neighborhood church is no longer a reality in American life. Most people today drive past several churches, often one or more from their own denomination, in order to reach the one they attend. Lyle Schaller suggests the need for a congregation to move beyond thinking about their church as a geographical parish, and observes that many people today are willing to travel fifteen to forty minutes to church. [6]

The development of a ministry plan requires gathering information, including data about people who live within driving distance of the church. Several commercial vendors provide detailed information of great benefit to a church on a wide range of census data, including such things as the number of single adults under thirty-five and the number of families with preschool children. In addition, a good deal more data is available on such subjects as education, income level, housing types, and even lifestyle patterns.[7] Additional material on people in your community may be obtained from such sources as the city government, a metropolitan newspaper, and the local library.

It will also be helpful to do a community survey. This need not be a complex or intimidating process. A random sampling of perhaps one hundred community residents will provide considerable information which will help the task force assess the work of the church and suggest areas which need to be examined. George Barna lists questions which may guide the task force in preparing a brief questionnaire: "Are people aware of the church? Do they understand what it stands for? What is the general impression of the congregation? Does it seem relevant and contemporary?  If a person was interested in attending a church, what are the chances he would consider that particular church?  What issues and personal needs should the church be addressing in its services and programs?"[8]

When a community survey is being taken, those who conduct it should introduce themselves and their church and then say something like this:  "Would you mind taking two or three minutes to give us your opinions about the church?"  Most people will be happy to do so.  Saturday morning is generally a good time to take such a survey.

In addition to assessing information from the community, the task force needs to do some analysis of the congregation in an effort to discover what is presently working well. Once again, a survey may be the best way to gather that information.  Barna suggests having "all members and visitors who attend the church complete a questionnaire at a single point in time (e.g. on a predetermined Sunday morning)."[9]  The questionnaire is to provide an opportunity for people to describe their feelings about their church involvement, their evaluation of the effectiveness of the church's services and programs, their opinions about the adequacy of the church's resources and facilities, and their expectations for the future.  From the results of the congregational survey, the task force will be able to identify areas in which the church does well, things which need to be improved, and issues for future development.

As with all information gathering, someone needs to take the raw data and summarize it, making it possible for the material to be readily accessible to the task force to guide it in its next steps.

With the research and information gathering tasks complete, the task force is now ready to begin writing a ministry plan. How much will be written is up to the task force, but in all church reports, brevity is beautiful.

Barna suggests that the first step in the writing stage is to restate the mission of the church. Writing this out is essential, for it enables everyone to be clear about the congregation's purpose and intentions. It also enables the congregation to keep focused on its ministry and to evaluate program strategies and proposals in light of what the church is committed to do in the service of Christ's kingdom.

The second step in writing the ministry plan is to summarize the results of the research about the community and the congregation. It will be helpful to include a summary of objective information about the past three to five years in the life of the church in terms of membership statistics, worship attendance, contributions, etc. A description of current outreach activities, along with their focus and results, should be included. This part of the report will provide the basis for an action plan.

The task force is now ready to list the needs and opportunities before the church. These will be ministry opportunities of significance which the church has the capacity to address. It will be helpful if the task force prioritizes this list. Doing so will allow for the development of a workable plan. A church cannot do everything, nor can it do everything at once. A plan with priorities challenges the congregation to begin now to be involved in ministry and to be prepared to continue to make advances as new opportunities and resources become available.

The third step in the development of the ministry plan is setting goals and objectives. Not everyone uses those terms in the same way. As used here, a goal is a statement of intent which sets forth what one hopes to accomplish. In the seminar, "How to Diagnose and Renew Your Church," Robert Orr suggests that goals are effective when they have the following characteristics: 1) they are *measurable*; 2) they are *attainable*; 3) they are *consistent with the stated purpose* of the church; 4) they have an action verb (*what* will be done) and a date (*when* it will be done); and, 5) they are *controllable* (that is, they specify action over which the church actually has control over and can do something about).[10]

Lyle Schaller has observed an important distinction between "survival goals" and "mission goals."[11] Survival goals focus on problems and are remedial. They tend to discourage new initiatives in ministry since they are primarily concerned with the maintenance of the institution. Mission goals look at new possibilities for ministry, and are usually innovative and future-oriented. They focus on the needs of people, and have the added benefit of enlisting a high level of support within the church from both newcomers and older members. A ministry plan calls for mission goals.

Goals are addressed through "objectives." An objective is a statement of method which sets forth a specific means by which the goal will be reached. Let's look at an example. In the research process, it was discovered that, while the church attracts a significant number of first-time visitors in worship, not many return for a second visit. Several goals could be developed in response to that need. One might be that within six months, one-third of first time visitors will be returning for a second visit. What objectives could be developed in response to that goal?

As the task force works to form objectives, the question they must deal with is: What must happen in the church if this goal is to be realized? That involves looking at the worship service, as well as the congregation's attitude toward and reception of worship visitors. Objectives might be developed in either or both of those areas. The committee will also need to consider visitor follow up. In that specific area several objectives could be developed. Perhaps the task force will suggest these two: to immediately begin registering worship attendance so that all visitors can be identified; and, within one month, have a system which assures that all first-time visitors receive a telephone call on the day of their visit to express appreciation for their attendance and to encourage them to return.

Goals and objectives are likely to be no more than words on paper unless one more step is taken. Some steps must be developed to implement the objectives. What resources and methods will be used in carrying out these tasks, and who will be responsible to see that they are done? Determining specific courses of action is not a simple task. It is probably beyond the scope of the task force's mandate. I would like to suggest a possible approach.

When the task force has completed the development of its prioritized list of needs, with proposed goals and objectives, the task force report is presented to the church's governing board. The board will need to take adequate time to absorb this material. It may decide to circulate the report so that other members can respond before action is taken. When the board is ready to act, it decides which of the proposed goals will be adopted for the coming year. After consensus has been reached about the goals, they will be assigned, along with the proposed objectives, to an appropriate committee in the church. Each committee will be requested to report back to the board, as soon as possible, the objectives it will employ to achieve the approved goals. While the committee will first consider the objectives the task force has recommended, it will be free to propose new objectives in addition to or in place of the task force recommendations. The committee's recommended objectives will be presented to the board for approval, and after they are approved, the committee will be responsible for implementation. It is they who will decide the specifics of what will be done, as well as when and by whom.

When all selected goals and objectives have been approved, they may be reported to the congregation, along with periodic progress reports throughout the year.

An effective ministry plan will have the following features:

1. It will demonstrate that the congregational leadership is urging the adoption of a new agenda and is advocating changing the priorities of the church. In the great majority of congregations, the priority currently evident is ministry to the present membership. A ministry plan for evangelization creates and announces a new priority.

2. It will help the congregation recognize the price to be paid. A question sometimes asked by a church consultant is "What problems would an increase of one hundred (or two hundred) new members create for you?" The purpose in asking such a question is not simply to help the leadership identify potential needs, but to help them wrestle with the question of whether they are prepared to make the sacrifices and pay the increased costs which will certainly accompany a commitment to evangelization. The leadership owes it to the congregation to point out what some of the costs are likely to be, and to give people the opportunity to freely decide about their willingness to pay that price.

3. It will raise the level of expectations within the congregation. Members anticipate that new things will be happening, and that each person in the congregation will be challenged to help bring these goals to fulfillment. Committees who are working on objectives will be urged to develop and promote specific opportunities for church member's participation.

4. It will take seriously the need to communicate regularly to the congregation, and will provide a consistent supply of information on plans, progress, and results for each objective.

5. It will provide an opportunity for the congregation to give feedback throughout the process, and to be able to offer midcourse corrections. Perhaps the board will schedule several "talk-it-over" sessions to give people specific opportunities for evaluation.

When these suggestions are followed, criticism and disagreement will be substantially reduced. They cannot be eliminated, yet one should not be unduly concerned about that. It is the task of leaders to lead, and when they do so out of conviction and with an honest effort to encourage the congregation to embrace the vision as well, they need not agonize over a minority that refuses to cooperate. When leaders lead with conviction, by example, and out of a life of prayer, people will follow.

Prerequisite #4: *The Church Makes Evangelization a Priority*

Not long ago, I heard a pastor say he was working to make evangelism "one of the top priorities of our congregation." I respect that pastors desire to lift the place of evangelism in the life of his congregation, but his words made me wince a little. Perhaps I am too sensitive at this point, but I think making evangelism "one of our top priorities" is in fact a symptom of the problem in many churches.

What is a "top priority" anyway? A priority is that which takes precedence, or that which is given first consideration. If my priority with this week's paycheck is to pay the rent, that clearly implies that the rent will be the first thing I pay. If making a car payment is my "top priority," perhaps that means the first thing I will do when I get my paycheck is to make the car payment. We cannot have many priorities or we will be frozen in inactivity. Only one top priority is possible, for we cannot both pay the rent first and make our car payment first. *Only one thing* can truly have priority, which literally means "to come before."

Talking about making evangelism "one of our top priorities" suggests to me that we have not yet decided that evangelization is what God is calling us to do.

I believe it is. Without hesitation, I claim evangelization is to be our top priority. This does not mean other tasks of the church are of secondary importance. Worship, education, fellowship are foundational pillars. And the fourth pillar — mission — is much broader than evangelization. It includes feeding the hungry, visiting the imprisoned, and carrying out the other work Jesus said was the true evidence of his followers (Matthew 25:32-46). In calling for the priority of evangelization, we do not claim it as a ministry of superior value.

What we do claim is that evangelization is the first bill we must pay. Given the present situation in our churches and in our world, evangelization requires and deserves our greatest attention and the best of our resources.

It is my conviction that those churches which acknowledge such a priority — and only those churches — will be able to evangelize the baby boom generation.

[1] *Christian Century*, November 15, 1989.

[2] Herb Miller, *The Vital Congregation* (Nashville:  Abingdon Press, 1990), p. 106.

[3] Win Arn,  *The Church Growth Ratio Book.*  Monrovia: Church Growth Press, p. 43

[4] "Win Arn Growth Report" #25  Monrovia: Church Growth, Inc.

[5] Herb Miller, *The Vital Congregation* (Nashville:  Abingdon Press, 1990), p. 76.

[6] Lyle E. Schaller, *Choices for Churches* (Nashville:  Abingdon Press, 1990), p. 85.

[7] Church Growth, Inc. provides this service in a product called "Demographic Analysis of Your Community."  For more information call 1-800-423-4844.

[8] George Barna, *Marketing The Church* (Colorado Springs; NAVPRESS, 1988), p. 75.

[9] *Ibid.,* p. 74.

[10] The "How to Diagnose & Renew Your Church" seminar is sponsored by Church Growth, Inc., Monrovia, California, and offered on a regular basis in cities across the country.

[11] Lyle Schaller. "Problems or Possibilities?" *Church Administration.*  The Sunday School Board of the Southern Baptist Convention.  May, 1977, p. 45.

# CHAPTER SIX

# A Church Which Is Inviting

Not long ago, the Alban Institute released a study of new member assimilation called *The Inviting Church*.[1] It is an excellent work, one well worth reading. Note the title, with its imaginative play on words. Churches which do well in incorporating newcomers are sure to be inviting, in the sense of being attractive and appealing. They are also inviting in the sense of welcoming and encouraging participation. Congregations which hope to attract baby boomers will be inviting in both ways.

In my opinion, the single most important discovery of the church growth movement is that personal invitations extended by church members are the primary means by which newcomers are brought to church. Study after study has confirmed that more than three-quarters of all adults who join a congregation are first brought to that church by a friend or relative. Win Arn was one of the early proponents of this important insight. [2]

Lyle Schaller describes congregations which are effectively inviting: "The congregations in which members invite others to come to church with them usually display these characteristics: (a) the members are enthusiastic about their faith as Christians, (b) the members are enthusiastic about this congregation, (c) the members are enthusiastic about the current pastor, (d) the congregation as a whole conveys the expectation that members will invite others to come to church with them, (e) most of the members actively and enthusiastically greet and welcome visitors, and (f) that particular program or, if it is on Sunday morning, that worship experience is planned on the assumption that first-time visitors will be present." [3]

We cannot assume that inviting will take place automatically. The fourth item on Schaller's list merits special attention — "The congregation conveys the expectation that members will invite others to come with them." The practice of extending invitations flows out of the vision of the church as an evangelizing community. As that vision is communicated, members of the congregation are encouraged to participate by inviting their friends to church. In the development of a ministry plan, special occasions for inviting may be scheduled and promoted. Many congregations celebrate "Invite-A-Friend" Sundays, and announce them far enough in advance so that members can pray and plan an approach to their friends.[4]

In a strategy for reaching baby boomers, invitations to attend church events are particularly important. As we shall discuss again, the key role here will be played by members of the congregation who are themselves baby boomers. Those members have contacts with their cohorts outside the church and understand how best to approach and invite their friends.

A second area in which inviting is necessary is in invitations to explore faith. Robert Gribbon recently wrote *Developing Faith In Young Adults*, which updates his research with 18 to 35-year-olds. The group he has studied only partially overlaps the baby boom generation, but one of his discoveries is of great importance, and is, in my judgment, equally true for older boomers. Gribbon talks about young adults approaching the church tentatively, as if to test both themselves and the church. His discovery is that "a majority come seeking commitment rather than as a result of commitment."[5] That is significant; an evangelizing congregation must understand this reality and respond to it. The church needs to help its members learn to talk about their faith. A survey taken in one denomination found only 16 percent of church members felt comfortable sharing their faith.[6] The same study revealed that many people wanted to do so, but felt they did not know how. Congregations need to provide practical training in this area.

The baby boom generation is not likely to be reached by those who have learned a packaged evangelism presentation. Baby boom seekers often come to faith slowly, and those who are seeking to reach them in their journey must also travel slowly. In that process, baby boom believers will have opportunities to winsomely talk about their spiritual values. The evangelizing congregation needs to help its members understand the development of their own faith journeys, and discover ways to describe the process to others. Providing such learning experiences is essential.

An evangelizing congregation should also provide public occasions in which faith issues are explored. Some congregations regularly schedule an event which is sometimes called an "Inquirer's Class." The idea of such a gathering is to give people an opportunity to explore the Christian faith, to raise questions about it, and to consider their own response. This is not to be confused with a pre-membership class, in which participants are on the road to joining the church. Rather, this gathering is completely open-ended. One assumes that at its conclusion some who have participated will make no further response. It is designed for those who are exploring faith and is a place where any faith question can be raised, any doubt expressed. It is an event to which members of the congregation can invite seeking — or skeptical — friends, and come with them as they test the waters of faith.

"Inviting" also involves encouraging further involvement of those who have come to a worship service or a church function. This task should be carried out, not primarily by the people who brought them to the event, but by church members who met them there. An important assumption is that whenever the congregation gathers, people will socialize and introduce the visitors they have brought. This provides an opportunity for newcomers to meet other people of similar age and interests who will extend invitations to participate in groups or activities in which they are involved.

The importance of these invitations becomes clear when we realize that the path by which people generally move into the church is the smaller groups and activities of the congregation. In an adult education class, a choir, or a golf league, friendships are formed and lives are changed. That begins to happen for newcomers as they are invited to participate in such groups and activities.

A congregation seeking to reach baby boomers is one which extends invitations. What else is characteristic of an inviting church?

## *A Church That Attracts Baby Boomers Has a Warm Climate*

A congregation effective in ministry with the boom generation will be a warm and friendly place. That atmosphere will be apparent in the welcome extended to newcomers. Not only will the congregation show a willingness to accept new people, but a delight in it. The hospitality of such a church is evident in the greeting visitors receive, in the signs that provide direction (clearly intended for them), in the welcome given by verbal announcement and in printed bulletin, and in the provision made for them to fully participate in the service or events for which they came.

The friendliness of the congregation will be particularly apparent through the individual greetings by members. At least five people should come up to a visitor, introduce themselves, and spend a moment welcoming him/her. These are not information-seeking conversations, and so questions are not asked of the newcomer. Church members are sensitive to evidence of discomfort in some newcomers, who may not be used to such attention, and avoid adding to that discomfort. In conversations with visitors, church members seek to introduce themselves, repeat the name of the visitor when they hear it, thank the person for coming, and invite him/her to return. If appropriate, an invitation to some other event may be given.[7]

This kind of welcoming does not come without effort. In many churches, worship visitors are virtually ignored. A friend of mine recently described her experience in attempting to make her way into a new congregation. She has a reason for wanting to be part of that church, but is very frustrated about the coldness she has experienced. After five or six visits, she told me, not a single person, other than an official greeter, has spoken to her. "I could drop over dead walking into that place," she said, "and people would just go on by."

An active and gracious welcome does not just happen; it is a result of a recognition of the importance and the duty of hospitality, a decision to be an intentionally welcoming community, and implementing specific actions.

The warmth and friendliness of a congregation is evident in other ways. It may be seen not only in the lively conversations taking place after an event has ended, but in the way people in these groups open their circle to include others. It is demonstrated in people's efforts to learn and remember names. It is evident in the growing depth of personal relationships within the church family.

When first time visitors return for a second visit, it is primarily a result of the welcome they experienced when they attended previously.

*A Church That Attracts Baby Boomers Has an Open Environment*

An evangelizing congregation is open to new people. That is apparent when churches demonstrate that its doors are open wide for all who wish to enter. Are the doors open for baby boomers?

Some of those who wish to enter will be different than those who are inside. They will dress differently. Some will be of different races and colors. They will live by different values, and have different life styles. Some will be living together outside of marriage. Some will be poor. They will not agree with all our doctrines and will not accept all the ways we do things. They may speak a different language, and challenge some of ours. They will ask questions, and want to know "why" about many things that are comfortable and familiar to us. Are the doors of our church going to stay open for them? Can we accept all this change and variety, and these people who are different than we are?

It may help to remember that "acceptance" is not the same as "approval." It is possible to welcome and love people who do things we do not condone. Our task is to accept and care for people, it is God who creates change. Our loving acceptance may bring people into the church's fellowship and encourage them to stay, and in so doing to allow them to be part of a community where God's Word is heard, God's Spirit is active, and God's love is changing people.

That is only part of the story. Being open to the baby boom means a willingness to accept diversity, and to be tolerant of differences. Even Christian baby boomers will be unlike other members, and evangelizing their generation requires a willingness to overlook some differences and accept others. That is part of the price to be paid.

An open environment includes being open to new styles. A church in ministry with the baby boom will learn to do its ministry in some new ways. It will need to get past the seven last words of the church — "we never did it that way before." New styles may be called for in leadership, moving away from an authoritarian model to a more open and participatory style. A more simplified structure may be called for. Baby boomers seem not to care much about the institutional aspects of church life, and are impatient with bureaucracy, red tape, and organizational structures. The church needs to be open to rethink, revise, and remove structures if necessary. The goal is ministry, not institutional requirements.

An open environment involves a willingness to trust people, to operate by consensus, to be informal and flexible. Churches which manifest this style give people permission to carry out new aspects of ministry with a minimum of institutional control. They encourage the development of new forms of ministry, and their attitude to such initiatives is to say "Great! How can we help you?"

A church seeking to evangelize the baby boom generation is open to new directions in ministry. Specific illustrations of such new directions will be dealt with in the following chapter. There are, however, principles which prepare us to be open to new program directions. One principle is that God works in new ways, and we must be open to new discoveries of that in our congregations. Our churches must listen for the whisper of the fresh winds of the Spirit. A second principle is that the baby boom represents a new way of life, and old methods are not proving effective in reaching them. That should lead us to hold our traditions lightly, and to be willing to accept change.

Lyle Schaller has written about an important principle for introducing change. It involves operating with a "both-and" approach, rather than an "either-or." An either-or approach always creates winners and losers, but a both-and approach can generally result in winners all around. An illustration of the difference may be helpful. A congregation for many years has had an adult Bible study group at church on Wednesday nights. At one time, more than fifty people regularly attended, but it has slipped over the years and now gets twelve to fourteen people, most of them over the age of sixty. The class has always been taught by the pastor.

Recently,a few younger adults approached the pastor about starting a Thursday morning Bible study group at 6:30 in a neighborhood restaurant. Since it would be difficult for the pastor to do both, the proposal which comes to the church board is to discontinue the Wednesday evening group and begin a new one in its stead. A disadvantage of this either-or approach is that it cancels an activity which apparently has value for more than a dozen people. A both-and approach involves a decision to have two Bible study groups. Not only does that eliminate causing pain to a group of faithful church members, it has the advantage of increasing the number of people who will be involved in Bible study. Of course, a solution still must be found for the pastor's schedule problem. Perhaps a both-and solution can be found for that problem, as well.

Not all problems have easy solutions, but looking at the both-and option nearly always benefits the congregation. It makes dealing with change less painful, it increases choices, and that makes for effective ministry.

A congregation with an open environment opens the door for new leadership. That means a willingness to bring younger members into leadership positions. In his study of ministry with people in the 18 to 40 age group, Robert Gribbon points out the importance of providing both opportunity and support for their leadership. "Young adults want to do a good job. To do so, they need to know what is expected, freedom to do the job, support from peers and leaders, and freedom to fail or back out gracefully if needed." [8]

Evangelizing congregations are not only willing to bring younger members into leadership positions, but new members as well. Baby boomers are attracted to congregations in which leadership includes young members, women, and newer members. Growing churches will generally have half the membership of their governing board made up of persons who have joined the congregation within the past five years.

Finally, an open environment includes welcoming and responding to criticism. Open churches encourage people to evaluate the ministry taking place and give attention to comments and suggestions from those involved in, or affected by, that ministry. Ministry efforts are improved by seeking such responses and giving careful consideration to them.

## A Church That Attracts Baby Boomers Has A Clear Identity

Churches with a clear identity know who they are, why the are in that community, and what God is calling them to do. Their identity is evident in the way the congregation lives and carries out its ministry.

Identity may be shaped by an existing strength of the congregation, or by a sense of call. No matter how it originates, the identity fits the church and is consistent with its purpose, strengths, and opportunities. The identity is understood and affirmed by the members of the church and is a focus of the congregation in its evangelizing activities.

One congregation I am familiar with identified its strength as being a caring community. A decision was made to intentionally build on this strength, and a church logo was designed which incorporated this theme. The leaders affirmed this strength continually, expressing gratitude for it and encouraging church members and groups to manifest this quality. Caring seemed to increase as a result, and new program initiatives emerged. People in the congregation talked with one another about their caring community, and spoke about it to those with whom the church was in ministry. Years later, when people described this church, they almost always spoke of it in terms of being a caring community. Such is the power of an intentional ministry focus.

"Identity" and "focus" grow out of a congregation's self-understanding. How is your church different from the one down the street? What do you do well? Are you capitalizing on your present strengths? What emphasis seems of greatest urgency in your congregation right now? Is there something the congregation recognizes God is calling it to be or do? Answering such questions helps identify a church's uniqueness. Adopting that uniqueness as a focus of ministry provides opportunity to move forward in a clear direction, and that gives the congregation a clear identity.

*A Church That Attracts Baby Boomers Relates To Its Community*

While few congregations these days are neighborhood churches, no congregation can have an effective ministry if it ignores its neighborhood. A church which is attractive to the baby boom is one which relates well to its community. At least three important ingredients may be seen when a church effectively relates to its community.

First, the congregation seeks to enhance relationships with people who live in the immediate neighborhood. Some churches give the impression of being completely indifferent to their community and take no steps to relate. Few of their members live in the area of the church. Almost all such churches are in decline and will eventually die.

Other congregations take actions which enhance relationships. They make their facilities available to the community for special events and activities. They encourage the use of their building for weddings and other kinds of gatherings. These decisions are not made in order to increase the church's income. Ideally, no charge should be made for the use of the building, with the possible exception of a minimal contribution to offset actual expenditures.

Some churches provide professional counseling services, which the congregation underwrites. Other congregations periodically invite neighborhood people to share a meal. One congregation annually invites its neighbors to an ice cream social on the church

lawn, which it calls "Sundaes on Tuesday." A
church in New Jersey sponsors a community
Christmas carol sing.  In addition to such
activities, pastors of inviting churches spend
time in the community, and are visibly
present.

A second component in a good church-to-
community relationship is the church's
involvement in concerns important to the
community.  A congregation may find a
neighborhood organization already active and
working on concerns which enhance the life of
its residents.  If no such group exists, the
church may want to consider working toward
bringing one into being.  In any case, the
church can be an active partner with other
concerned citizens and work on needs in the
community.  Surely the church will find people
who are actively involved in addressing issues
and concerns which are also important to the
church.

A third aspect of involvement occurs when
a congregation identifies a specific need in the
community and develops a response to it.  In
taking a neighborhood survey, one
congregation asked this question:  "Are you
aware of any needs in this community which
are not presently being met?"  A number of
people responded by talking about the children
who were on the streets from the time school
was dismissed until parents returned home
from work.  As a result, that church developed
an after-school program which provided an
important ministry opportunity and bridge to
the community.

Other congregations have created neighborhood food pantries or clothing banks, refurbished neighborhood housing, sponsored clean-up campaigns, worked to get rid of pornography or drugs, tutored neighborhood children, and even built low-cost housing units. In each case, specific neighborhood programs were initiated in response to discovered areas of need. A baby boomer friend of mine described her frustration one time by remarking, "The church is good at pointing out problems in our world, but not very good in helping us find ways to do something about them." Programs such as the ones described here are illustrations of ways the church can make a difference. Developing such creative programs helps churches enlist the gifts of members, particularly baby boom members, in doing something about problems. Bridges are then built with baby boomers outside the church who share a concern to address such needs.

This is not to suggest that ministry is undertaken in order to improve the community's image of the church, or in order to make contacts for evangelizing. Community ministry is part of the mission of the church, and is an end in itself. It is true, however, that faithfulness in this area demonstrates integrity and validates the church's mission. That enhances its evangelizing ministry with baby boomers who are looking for genuiness and authenticity.

*A Church That Attracts Baby Boomers Cares About Its Facilities*

Many people form their initial impressions of a church from the first sight of the church's facilities. What impression do you think someone would form of your congregation if they saw your building for the first time today? Would they think of your church as "inviting"?

Certain impressions are gained from the church's architecture, and from the age and size of the buildings. Perhaps not much can be done about those things, but then, they are not the most important, either. Of greater significance is evidence that the people of the congregation take pride in their church and want others to find it welcoming. That desire is expressed, for example, in the church's sign, in the careful maintenance of the property and buildings, in the parking lot, the sidewalks, the flower gardens.

An inviting church is also apparent inside the building. Here too, a welcoming climate is evident in signs providing directions for newcomers, in attractive posters and banners, and in the concern for cleanliness and neatness. Good impressions can be achieved by every congregation, no matter what its size or the extent of its resources.

Did you know that baby boomers have higher expectations for a church's facilities than their parents do? Lyle Schaller points out that a decision to reach younger people usually requires both more extensive and higher quality facilities. "A new generation of people have come on the scene who expect attractive nurseries, air-conditioning, excellent acoustics, convenient off-street parking, carpeted rooms, comfortable chairs, attractive rest rooms, and many other amenities of life that were considered luxuries in the earlier years of the twentieth century."[9]

Two items on Schaller's list warrant additional comment. First, a word about the church nursery. Congregations hoping to reach the baby boom generation must make their nursery first rate. Baby boom parents are not going to become part of a church that appears to neglect its children. Church nurseries must be clean, well-ventilated, adequate in size, generously equipped, and staffed with the best the church can provide. This is one place churches cannot afford to compromise.

Another area of importance is off-street parking. Like it or not, baby boomers consider ease of accessible parking an important factor in their selection of a church. Herb Miller suggests that a test of adequacy is whether the church's off-street parking, along with the street parking immediately adjacent to the property, provides spaces equal to half the worship attendance at the congregation's morning service (or at the largest service if the church has more than one).[10] Authorities from Church Growth Inc. suggest a rate of one parking space for every 1.75 people in worship.

Reviewing the adequacy of facilities is discouraging for people in churches where the facilities are obviously inadequate. Many congregations are located in buildings that are old or the wrong size. Rather than giving in to discouragement, it is good to take positive action. Begin by objectively evaluating your facilities, keeping in mind the points which have been made. Develop a list of the concerns that emerge from that evaluation. Remember that recognizing a problem is the first step toward resolving it. Review your list, and as each need comes up, ask two questions: Is there something here we can correct? Is there something here for which we can compensate?

Correcting might involve purchasing additional property to enlarge the facility or the parking lot. More commonly, it means clean-up and fix-up projects, such as doing some painting, renovating the nursery, trimming the shrubbery, and replacing the sign in front of the building. Quite a few corrective steps can be taken with minimal financial cost.

Compensating takes imagination. What can be done, for example, where a church has insufficient off-street parking and correcting that situation is not feasible? Possibilities vary with communities, but options might include: parking spaces near the building marked "Reserved for Visitors," church leaders setting an example by not using the parking lot, arranging for parking at a distance and providing shuttle service to the church building, making arrangements with a nearby commercial parking lot to provide parking at a special rate, advertising that two subway tokens or bus tickets will be given to worship visitors upon request. Compensating involves developing creative alternatives when an existing problem cannot be solved.

Churches which appeal to people in the 25 to 45 age group display the following traits.

*They Give Attention to the Central Religious Task of the Church.*

In his research on baby boomers who are returning to church, Robert Gribbon found that many of those making their way back had difficulty expressing just why they were returning, or what they were looking for in the church. Gribbon suggests, "they primarily look to the church as a place to find religion, to worship, to 'practice and fulfill my faith.'"[11] In an earlier study, Gribbon had reported: "The signs are clear that people are looking for spiritual depth from the church and are critical when they do not find it. People are looking for authenticity in the church and the clergy."[12]

Gribbon's research points out that congregations involved in ministry with the baby boom need to center that ministry in spiritual meaning, and the development of the spiritual life. Program suggestions will be offered in the next chapter, but none of them can be placed on the same level of importance as this. The primary evangelizing task of the church is to provide encouragement and assistance to those who are seeking to develop or deepen a relationship with God, and to support a movement toward wholeness and maturity in Christ.

*They are Committed to Excellence.*

In his book *Help! I'm A Baby Boomer*, Hans Finzel writes, "My personal observation is that many baby boomers who are committed to excellence in their work are turned off by the shabbiness that characterizes many local churches."[13]  I am convinced that Finzel is right.  Baby boomers cannot be expected to put up with slipshod work.  They are alienated by such experiences as receiving a worship bulletin with misspelled words, or with lines of type running on angles down the page.  Poorly planned worship services, ill-conceived and irrelevant sermons, musicians who cannot accompany congregational singing, last Sunday's bulletin still on the pew today, and sound systems that either do not work or have not been adjusted prior to the service are all unacceptable to baby boomers.

Personally, I think people are right to be offended by such practices. Are we content to offer such shoddiness to God?  All churches ought to strive for excellence.  If a church cannot do something well, or find someone who can do it well, perhaps it would be better not to do it.

*They are Willing to Challenge People.*

It has been recognized that "high demand" churches are often very effective in evangelization.  High demand churches set forth challenging expectations for member-ship.  Requirements vary with congregations, but whatever the specific expectations, two points should be recognized.  Such churches do not hesitate to issue challenges, because they understand that big challenges have the power to generate big commitments. Also, these churches are clear about their expectations from the beginning and do not attempt to hide them. They are not afraid to challenge people.

*They are Oriented to the Baby Boom Environment.*

- They are culturally oriented, and sensitive to the values, needs, and concerns of the people they seek to serve.
- They are experientially oriented, and provide ministry which stresses Christianity for practical living.
- They are future oriented, and more interested in planning for what can happen tomorrow than recapturing what happened yesterday.
- They are growth oriented, and therefore see the church's mission in terms of those who do not yet believe and belong.
- They are people oriented, and therefore more interested in people than programs, institutions, and buildings.
- They are action oriented, and therefore committed to doing rather than talking.

Because of all this and through all of this, they are inviting. And inviting churches are effective in ministry with the baby boom generation.

1 Roy M. Oswald and Speed B. Leas, *The Inviting Church* (Washington: The Alban Institute, 1987).

2 Win Arn, *The Master's Plan For Making Disciples*, (Pasadena: Church Growth, Inc., 1982) p. 43.

3 Lyle E. Schaller, "Where Are The Visitors?" (*Church Management — The Clergy Journal*, April, 1984), p. 147.

4 One excellent planning kit which has been developed to help a church conduct a successful "invite a friend" Sunday is entitled "Celebration of Friendship." It is available from Church Growth, Inc., (2670 S. Myrtle Ave. #201, Monrovia, CA 91016; 818-447-2112).

5 Robert T. Gribbon, *Developing Faith In Young Adults* (Washington: The Alban Institute, 1990), p. 33.

6 The survey was taken in the United Church of Christ, and is entitled "The Soundings Project: 1988-1989."

7 A helpful manual entitled, "How to Help Greeters Extend a Warm and Friendly Welcome" will help greeters and other members in this area. It is available from Church Growth, Inc., Monrovia, CA.

8 Robert T. Gribbon, *Half The Congregation: Ministry with 18 to 40 Year Olds* (Washington: The Alban Institute, 1984), p. 13.

9 Lyle E. Schaller, *Choices For Churches*, (Nashville: Abingdon Press, 1990), p. 94.

10 Herb Miller, *The Vital Congregation*, (Nashville: Abingdon Press, 1990), p. 42.

11 Gribbon, *Half The Congregation*, p. 28.

12 Robert T. Gribbon, *Thirty Year Olds and the Church: Ministry with the Baby Boom Generation* (Washington: The Alban Institute, 1981), p. 16.

13 Hans Finzel, *Help! I'm A Baby Boomer* (Wheaton: Victor Books, 1989). p. 144.

# CHAPTER SEVEN

# A Church That Works

In this chapter we will consider some of the activities at which congregations must work to successfully carry on ministry with the baby boom generation.

## THE CHURCH WORKS AT UNDERSTANDING BABY BOOMERS

In the opening chapters, we gave considerable attention to understanding this unique generation. We gained an awareness of the impact of baby boomers on our society and of society's effects upon them. We relived some of the attitudes, experiences, and events which shaped their identity. We considered the issues, concerns, and needs evident in their lives today. We studied their struggles, values, and hopes.

Gaining information is an important first step, but it does not assure understanding. That comes as new knowledge touches our emotions, forming attitudes of empathy and understanding. Only when such identification occurs can we be effective in ministry with baby boomers.

Understanding this generation allows us to plan ministry efforts based upon identified interests and needs. The church exists to serve the needs of people, and only as needs are recognized and understood can appropriate responses be made. These responses must address the issues baby boomers are struggling with and the goals they are striving for, or they will not be effective. An evangelizing congregation endeavoring to reach baby boomers works at understanding them, and since understanding is never complete, the process of working at it is continuous.

One issue that needs to be understood is why the church has missed so many of the baby boom generation.

The height of the church's popularity in the United States corresponds almost exactly with the baby boom's birth years. Huge numbers of that generation were in churches and Sunday schools as children — certainly a higher percentage than of any other generation in American history. Yet approximately two-thirds of them left the church. Why?

In one sense, that may not be the right question. It is not unusual for young people growing into adulthood and experiencing independence to drift away from church. Ordinarily after a period of time they make their way back and recover their religious roots. With the baby boom, however, many drifted away and did not return — more than one-third of those who left, according to research done by Roof and McKinney.[1] A better question, then, is why did they not come back?

Answering that question requires looking at several different factors. Events in their life experiences, as we have seen, led many to a rejection of parental values, a distrust of institutions, a spirit of skepticism, and a quest for personal fulfillment. Feelings and attitudes like these worked against a return to church.

Other influences in their lives and in society had a similar effect. Educational experiences led some to question their faith. The cultural pluralism which emerged so strongly in the 1960s gave rise to the idea that all truth is relative, and this worked against commitment and church involvement. Just about the time older boomers reached the age at which dropouts could be expected, the church's popularity took a nose-dive which had an added detrimental effect on their eventual return. Upon reaching adulthood, mobility increasingly took them away from their roots, and made church involvement less likely.

One more reason might be suggested. A new attitude about religion has emerged in American society. It is an attitude which the baby boom has helped create. *People have come to accept the separation of believing and belonging.* In the survey taken by Roof, there was compelling evidence of the trend to separate faith and church. Asked whether it is possible to be a good Christian without going to church, 95 percent of the boomers said it is.[2] When that attitude prevails, church involvement is sure to be affected.

Evidence indicates that the majority of baby boomers who are outside the church have not abandoned faith. The Roof McKinney study reports that 63 percent of the dropouts "consider themselves good Christians."[3] For many, it is not faith which has been left behind but the church. It seems certain that the church itself contributed to the baby boom's low level of involvement. What was it in the church that estranged so many?

Different answers are given to that question. Christian baby boom researcher Jack Sims says baby boomers react against some churches because of:

- individualism, and their dislike of rigid structure;
- different tastes in music;
- experiencing the church as boring, irrelevant, or high-pressured;
- being turned off by appeals for money; and
- finding these churches one-sided politically.[4]

Robert Gribbon reports on a study of young adults which asked them to identify ways in which organized religion was failing to do the job it should. The following reasons were given:

- Fails to meet the needs of people;
- Apathetic, uninspired;
- Too materialistic, too preoccupied with money;
- Out of date, out of touch with reality;
- Doesn't reach young people;
- Too many hypocrites; too smug; not true faith;
- Doesn't dig into the real problems facing humankind.[5]

In his most recent work, Gribbon describes conversations with young adults in which they were asked why some of their friends don't go to church. The answers given can be divided into three categories: some don't go because of negative experiences with the church, such as finding the church to be irrelevant, or being turned off by something experienced in church; some don't go because it has never been part of their lives; and some don't go because they do not feel a need. [6]

Since it is apparent that the church itself is part of the problem, church leaders need to identify attitudes and practices in their congregations which must be examined, and explore ways to provide ministry with the baby boom which avoids the mistakes of the past.

Church leaders also will want to understand why many baby boomers are making their way back into the church. We have noted three primary needs which bring most: a search for spiritual meaning; a hunger for community; and a desire for support with life tasks, particularly family concerns. In addition, Gribbon says most of those who return do so after a life transition such as the birth of a child, a divorce, or other life change. He also points out that invitations to participation were the means of return for most. [7]

Congregations wishing to be in ministry with the baby boom generation will want to look carefully at their own church through the eyes of this age group.

## THE CHURCH WORKS AT COMMUNICATING WITH BABY BOOMERS

Communication is a primary task of the church and is always important. But perhaps with no group is communication of greater importance than with "information-hungry" baby boomers. Before exploring avenues of communication, it helps to recognize some principles for presenting messages to this generation.

Baby boomers tend to be skeptical, so communication needs to avoid generalities and exaggerated claims while striving for truth and authenticity. Boomers are contemporary, so communications must use up-to-date images and graphics, avoid stereotypes, and make use of modern instruments. They are interested in learning, so we need to provide factual data as clearly and concisely as possible (since they are also in a hurry). Baby boomers are pragmatic, so communication needs to make clear the benefits and results of what is being offered. They are committed to excellence, so quality is crucial.

Before a communication piece is developed, attention must be directed to the communication channel or method which will be used. What strategy or style is most appropriate? Each communication piece needs to be prepared in light of these questions:

• Who is the audience?
• What do we want to help them understand?
• What obstacles do we need to overcome?
• How will they be addressed?
• What response are we seeking?

Communication takes place in two spheres: *external*, in which messages are sent to those who are not part of the church, and *internal*, in which the church communicates with its members. Since these are different audiences with different needs, it is unwise to send the same piece to both groups. Some congregations regularly send the church newsletter to people they are seeking to evangelize. That is unwise. A church newsletter, if sent only to constituents, can inform and challenge the congregation about issues of concern to members, such as how visitors are treated, or the current budget shortfall. It is preferable that such announcements be seen only by those who are members. Further, very few of the items typically included in church newsletters are of interest to those outside the church. The most important reason is that whatever is sent to persons who are not part of the church should be designed specifically for the circumstances and needs of such persons.

External communication involves advertising which encourages participation and seeks to enhance the image of the church. Advertising can be an effective ingredient in ministry with baby boomers. Spending 5 percent of the church's operating budget on advertising has been suggested as a norm for congregations serious about the evangelizing task. Since advertising is a complex field, a church is sure to benefit by seeking guidance from an advertising professional. If that is not possible, it is best to concentrate on one or two methods within the church's capability, do them well, and keep them up to date.

Advertising begins with the sign on the church property. Make it as attractive and appealing as possible. Advertisements in the yellow pages of the phone book are important, since the yellow pages are used primarily by people under age forty. Newspaper advertising is less effective with this age group, who do not spend much time reading a daily paper; although newspaper advertisements for Easter and Christmas services ought not be ignored. An advertisement in the newspaper's religion section is of almost no value in reaching unchurched baby boomers. Creative, well-done ads placed in other sections of the newspaper can be part of a church's "communication mix." Radio and television advertising will be available to and effective for some churches. All congregations should recognize the importance of utilizing a 24-hour answering machine which gives the time of services.

Direct mail is proving to be an effective strategy with some congregations reaching baby boomers. *The Boomer Report,* a newsletter on the baby boom generation, identifies direct mail as one of the most powerful tools to reach them, and adds that direct mail which makes the boomer feel special is particularly effective.[8] Success is directly proportional to the number of mailings sent out.

An article on direct mailing strategy in *Net Results*[9] suggests a mailing to 10,000 homes may be expected to draw between ten and forty people to a worship service. Suggestions for effectiveness include: postcards, so there is nothing that needs to be opened; offer something "free," if possible; mail at appropriate and seasonal times; point out a benefit to be obtained; and keep the message simple. Some congregations plan a year-long direct mail campaign. The most beneficial times to mail are at Easter, right after Labor Day, and at Christmas. Three other mailings might be planned: perhaps once in February, May, and October. Each piece should announce a special event or activity and invite participation. It is wise to mail at least six times per year to the same target group.

Every congregation needs an attractive, up-to-date brochure which describes the church and its program. Brochures which are most effective show pictures of people and contain clear and brief statements of the benefit people have found in belonging to the congregation. They list the services and programs which the church offers, with brief descriptions of their purpose and meeting times. They identify the ministry focus of the congregation, but do not attempt to tell everything about the church. Members of the congregation are encouraged to have several copies of the brochure on hand and give them to friends whom they have invited.

Congregations concerned about a positive image in their community will regularly submit material to local media on significant programs and activities in which the church is involved, particularly those which focus efforts on behalf of its immediate community. Creative church ministries that help people are newsworthy.

Perhaps you have seen one of the advertisements produced by the Episcopal Church. One shows a picture of King Henry VIII, with this caption: "In a church started by a man who had six wives, forgiveness goes without saying." A baby boomer who saw that would probably be brought up short by it, and perhaps stop to reflect on the message which follows: "Just as we all make mistakes, we can all be forgiven." The advertisement concludes with an invitation to join in the joy of worship and fellowship. Advertisements like these benefit the whole Christian community as they encourage positive attitudes toward the church.[10]

## THE CHURCH WORKS AT PROVIDING PROGRAMS TO REACH BABY BOOMERS

An important difference between baby boomers and their parents is in their first experience with a congregation. For most older adults, the initial visit to church is for a Sunday morning worship service. While that is also true for many baby boomers, for an increasing number it is not. "A large number of recent new members born after 1945 describe their first visit as coming to a weekday program, a Christmas eve service, or some event other than Sunday morning. The variety of possibilities is huge, but often includes the weekday nursery school, a Bible study group, aerobic dance classes, an athletic team, a play, a program designed for parents, a divorce recovery workshop, etc." [11]

Recognition of this pattern calls the church to two important tasks. First, an evaluation of existing groups and programs to be sure they are meeting the needs of present constituents, as well as actively seeking to incorporate newcomers. Second, to develop new groups and activities designed to reach people who are not presently part of the church fellowship. These programs are often called "entry events" because they are planned to provide avenues through which people may make their way into the life of the church. Any congregation desiring to be in ministry with the baby boom must provide such entry points. Specific programs need to be developed whose primary audience is those who live apart from the church. The more entry points a congregation can provide, the greater its potential for reaching the baby boom. While we may not be happy about it, they are very consumer-oriented, and go where their needs are met. That is true not just when they shop but also when they look at the church.

In planning programs for the baby boom generation, several principles should be kept in mind. First, options are important, and it is well to provide a diversified schedule which gives people choices. We can no longer assume that any one program will meet everyone's needs or appeal to the interests of all. Baby boomers are attracted by a variety of offerings in terms of alternative styles, different content and format, and a choice of schedule. Larger churches will have an advantage here, but virtually all congregations can increase the number of choices offered.

A second principle of program planning is to offer short-term events. Baby boomers tend to avoid long-term commitments, and prefer events which have a brief and concentrated focus. Ongoing programs should have a duration of perhaps four to eight weeks, with twelve weeks as an outside limit. Churches which schedule activities of relatively brief duration will find baby boomers more likely to participate.

A third principle in program planning is to promote convenience. That requires being sensitive to people's schedules and interests, and respecting their needs for space and time. Some churches have found that a one hour Saturday morning event, preceded by a continental breakfast, works well. Others are scheduling events in restaurants and offering a meal, or at church with a catered dinner. Churches willing to go to them, and adapt for them, are attracting baby boomers.

A fourth point about planning programs is to recognize that programs must have intrinsic value. Baby boomers do not go to events because they "should." Wade Clark Roof says that baby boomers "pick and choose with great care; the congregations that attract them must provide programs that have integrity and speak to their particular life experiences."[12] Quality is crucial. Whatever programs a church offers must be well planned and of high quality.

Now let's look at some types of programs which are being offered by congregations effective in ministry with the baby boom generation. One category of programs is called "seeker events." These are events which have a spiritual focus and are designed to provide exposure to the Christian life for those who have not made up their minds about it. Seeker events are designed for Christian baby boomers to attend with their unchurched friends. The purpose of such events must be communicated clearly, and adhered to strictly, with no surprises. Seeker events should conclude with an indication of the presenter's willingness to pursue the subject on a personal basis, such as, "If any of you wish to explore this further, please talk with me after the session about a time we can get together."

Seeker events come in a wonderful variety, from a restaurant dinner to a seminar, to a weekend retreat. They may involve several sessions on a selected topic such as: "Learning to read the Bible;" "Who is Jesus;" "Understanding Our Spiritual Journey;" or "Christianity and Other Religions." They may involve a guest speaker who discusses "Why I am a Christian." A seeker event could be planned as a Christian response to a current movie, best seller, or topic of interest. Seeker events provide an open environment in which faith issues can be presented without pressure.

A wonderful idea for a seeker event is reported in an article in *American Demographics* magazine. Credit for it is given to Jack Sims, who is introduced as "the president of B.O.O.M.E.R.S. (Believers Outside Of Most Every Religious System)."[13] Sims' event is called "Matthew's Party" and is held in the social room of a California health club. "Matthew's Party" is patterned after the events surrounding Jesus' call of Matthew to discipleship (Luke 5:27-32). In the joy of his new found relationship with Jesus, Matthew gave a party for his friends so that they could meet the Lord as well.

A Matthew's Party is an ideal seeker event. It could be held in a restaurant with members of the church who are baby boomers buying two tickets for the dinner, one for themselves and one for an unchurched friend. A speaker (perhaps a special guest) might give a brief talk on "How Jesus Christ Enriches Life." Several church members, prepared in advance, could give brief personal accounts of their own experience. A discussion time might follow. With this, as with all seeker events, the invitation to attend should make clear what the event will involve, and also assure guests they will not be asked to make any public response. The events are intended to help people in their search, not to manipulate them with contrived questions and answers.

A second category of programs designed for the baby boom are "issue-oriented events." These are programs sponsored by a congregation to provide support and assistance to people with their life tasks. As with seeker events, the format, style, and duration of the events may vary. The most common plan is a Saturday morning seminar or an evening class that meets four to six weeks. Family issues provide a host of options. Marriage enrichment can be addressed in a variety of topics such as, "What the Bible Teaches about Marriage," "Improving Communication in

Your Marriage," or "When the Honeymoon is Over — What Then?" Parenting classes can be scheduled for the parents of children in any age group or on a variety of parenting tasks.

A long list of other issues could be identified. Most of the concerns evident in the lives of people can be addressed by the church. A congregation could schedule events on such themes as learning money management, aging parents, preparing for marriage, mid-life issues, career changes, and so forth.

In planning issue-oriented events, churches should not overlook the opportunity to deal with life-transitions. Robert Gribbon's research has revealed that non-members do not generally seek the church during a time of crisis but after it has passed.[14] That points to program options which not only meet real needs but are geared to people who may be looking for church involvement. Programs could be planned for people dealing with the death of a spouse, recovering from divorce, living as singles, and dealing with issues of step-parenting or blended families. Any church could identify one such area in which to provide a quality event for people in the community.

Issue-oriented events have several positive benefits. They are intended primarily to meet human needs, to give practical help where it is needed, but they also foster relationships between members and non-members, demonstrate the church's concern for people, give understanding of how Christianity relates to daily life, and get people used to coming into the church building.

Some congregations will find it difficult to obtain the leadership necessary to provide a series of such events. Perhaps they could adopt the goal of scheduling two such events each year, one in the spring and one in the fall, one of which might be taught by the pastor and the other by a lay leader. In large congregations a variety of events may be offered throughout the year. A large church in Kirkland, Washington offers fifty such events each year.

In planning programs for people outside the church, a congregation does well to plan some things around the holidays, especially Christmas — the one time in the year that baby boomers are most likely to attend church.

It is helpful to look at some programs which are being used effectively in ministry with the baby boom. Let's begin with events for mothers. Nearly half of all new mothers stay home with their child during the first year of the child's life. This provides a great opportunity for a congregation looking for a ministry focus. Lyle Schaller identifies thirteen positive results of a church-sponsored Mother's Club, including: the formation of friendships, help with mothering tasks, providing a counterforce for postpartum blues, providing systematic Bible study, serving as an entry point for non-members, assimilating new members, and more. [15] Programs for new mothers are high on the list of attractive approaches for ministry with the baby boom generation.

A second program idea worth exploring is providing daycare or preschool services. While this meets a real need, it is only likely to be an effective "entry event" if church members are also active in this ministry and use it for inviting parents to other events. Otherwise, it has been shown to be of little value in the evangelization process of a church. That can take place if the church works at it. With the number of births showing an increase, the opportunity for such a service is great and will continue to be great throughout this decade.

Churches seeking to reach the baby boom need to plan programs designed specifically for that group, and each congregation must work to develop an effective program which it can do well. Planning such a program is best done by baby boomers who are already church members, so the program is planned by the people who most closely reflect the target audience.

## THE CHURCH WORKS AT PROVIDING EFFECTIVE MINISTRY

Three additional possibilities may enhance a congregation's ministry with the baby boom generation.

### The Role of Mentors

Gribbon's research with young adults indicates that "those whose journeys led them to involvement in a congregation often encountered both witnesses to a faith and facilitating persons who introduced them to a congregation."[16] People are likely to find their way into congregations when they meet inviters who open doors and hospitable persons who assist in entry and belonging. Congregations do well to encourage, develop, and affirm these gifts in their members. The more evident they are, the greater will be a congregation's effectiveness in evangelization.

The role of a mentor, however, is more than that. A mentor is a trusted counselor, guide, and role model. Mentors are men and women who display the grace and maturity of the Christian life in a winsome manner who have both an interest in and ability to provide assistance to others on their faith journeys. Mentors are usually older than the persons they serve, and the mentoring relationship is most commonly a one-to-one relationship.

Mentors can play a key role in ministry with the baby boom generation. Many boomers are separated from their parents by distance or circumstances. Perhaps parents can only rarely serve as mentors to their children, even if nothing separates them from each other. Often no extended family member is available to function as a mentor. Yet a mentor can be of great value to baby boom seekers who are looking for authenticity and for a Christian spirituality which is clearly genuine.

Recently, *Business Week* magazine devoted an issue to "The New America," in which they projected key trends of the 1990s.[17] In a section on "the young old," it was suggested that Americans over the age of 55 "could emerge as a key link in the social nexus of the 1990s" by serving as a "mentor generation." The article points out the need for such a role, the health and financial independence of many young seniors which

enables it, that generation's strong commitment to volunteering, and the benefit they
themselves would receive through feeling
wanted and needed.

Here is a great opportunity for the church:
to hold the vision of being mentors before the
young seniors in the church's fellowship, to
provide direction and encouragement for them
in this process, to facilitate the development of
relationships in which mentoring can take
place, to affirm where it is happening, and to
support this ministry with prayer.

## The Ministry of Small Groups

In almost every list of strategies suggested
for ministry with the baby boom generation, the
ministry of small groups will appear. Gribbon
provides a reason. "Part of what people look for
in a church is a sense of belonging, and this is
most frequently provided by face-to-face
encounter in which significant sharing can
take place."[18] Baby boomers are looking for
close personal relationships, and small groups
are one of the best ways the church can
respond to that need. Small groups provide for
the needs of both intimacy and support.

Generally, small groups are gatherings of
eight to twelve people who commit to meet
together on a regular basis (usually once a
week) for a specified period of time. Most
commonly they meet in the home of one of the
members. Participants are expected to make a
high commitment to the group which becomes,
in a real sense, their family. The groups are
usually led by laypersons.

The power of such groups became clear to me when I heard a baby boomer describe her experience.  She had lived apart from the church for some time and it was a small group which helped her to come back.  She spoke about how her faith had emerged and grown in the group, and movingly described the love and joy the members shared.  Since most of them had moved away from their roots, the group often spent their holidays together.  She related, almost in passing, that when one member of the group was unemployed for a time, everyone in the group contributed a "second tithe" to provide for family expenses until that person found work again.

It is clear that small groups can not only be an important means of socialization but of evangelization.  For evangelization to occur, of course, the groups need to have an influx of new and unchurched people.  If that is to take place a careful strategy needs to be developed and implemented.  That such an effort can be greatly successful is evident from Pastor Paul Cho's church in South Korea, a congregation built on small groups which now numbers over 600,000 members.  Some congregations in the United States are now using this model for growth.

Small groups can also be designed for educational purposes or as part of the process of incorporating new members.  Congregations interested in small group ministry need to identify the primary purpose of the groups and then provide training for leaders and appropriate resources which advance the church's goals.  While the format of groups may vary, the most common approach involves a combination of Bible study, personal sharing, and prayer. Small groups are proven to be very effective in building relationships.[19]

A cautionary word is advisable. Not everyone functions well in a small group. Some people are very uncomfortable with the intimacy and sharing which are a basic part of group life. It is unwise to assume that everyone will choose to participate in such groups. Since it is neither possible nor wise to convince people to do that which they resist doing, it must be recognized that small groups are not for everyone. That requires a congregation's leaders to develop alternative means of accomplishing the purpose for which the small groups are designed. Once again it is apparent that effective ministry involves offering choices.

## The Provision of Pastoral Care

For many baby boomers, a pastor has played an important role in their pilgrimage of faith and entry into the church. Gribbon reports "In almost every congregation visited there was a group of people who had been brought into the congregation directly through the pastor's contacts in the community."[20] For a church interested in reaching the baby boom, the potential is greatest where the pastor plays an active role in the evangelization ministry.

A good goal for pastors is to make at least 20 percent of pastoral calls on people who are not part of the congregation. Robert Orr, with Church Growth, Inc., suggests a creative concept that goes even farther: "pastoring the unchurched." He explains that it is an effective way to build a long-term relationship between a pastor and the unchurched person/family. The process is simple. It begins with the pastor going door to door in the neighborhood introducing him/herself as the pastor and asking whether the family has a person in their area they would call "their pastor." If they say, "no," the pastor asks whether they would mind if he/she could be their pastor. That doesn't mean they must go to church. It simply means that whenever their is a need in that family for "a pastor," they could call on him/her.

Once permission is gained, the pastor stays in regular contact with each of these new "members." (Some churches have an official designation called "constituent membership" for these persons.) A monthly visit to each home, regular letters, perhaps a gift book, etc. builds a trusting relationship with the pastor and family, so that if and when a need does arrive, the pastor is called.

Many churches have received new members as a direct result of pastoral calls on people who have recently moved into the community. The pastor's contact with community leaders, conversations at neighborhood events, participation in a service club, and greetings exchanged on neighborhood streets all provide opportunities for pastoral care. Pastors who make themselves available to the community will be sought out by people in the community when needs arise.

Four occasions of need commonly lead unchurched people to contact a pastor, and the more visible and approachable the pastor, the greater the number of such contacts. The occasions are: the desire for the pastor to perform a wedding; interest in having a child dedicated or baptized; a personal problem for which one seeks counsel; and a request for the pastor to conduct a funeral. Not all pastors will be able to respond positively to all such requests. Personal convictions and church requirements may make approval of some requests difficult or impossible.

However, it is possible to view all such requests as ministry opportunities. Further, a pastor can make a decision to agree to as many such requests as possible. That means that one should rarely, if ever, simply say "no" to such a request, especially over the telephone. A better approach is to suggest meeting with the person in order to discuss the request. In that meeting, pastoral care can be given. If the pastor is unable to do what is being asked, it may be possible to suggest alternatives. For the pastor committed to the ministry of evangelization, "yes" is the preferred answer to all requests for pastoral services.

If requests for pastoral services are to be ministry opportunities, they cannot also be accepted for the income they produce. In a fallen world one cannot, I suppose, indiscriminately offer such services at no charge. However, fees should be moderate when they are necessary, ought not be an early topic of discussion, nor the motivation for accepting the invitation. It will be important for the church board to discuss this matter. The board needs to make significant decisions regarding the pastor's role, provide adequate compensation for the pastor, and give compensatory relief from some parish responsibilities to allow the pastor the time to respond to ministry requests from persons outside the congregation's membership. Pastoral care need not be given only by pastors. Others have a role as well. However, it does begin with the pastor.

Pastoral care involves initiating opportunities for ministry as well as responding to them. Many life experiences provide opportunity for such ministry. Pastoral calls, cards and letters sent out, and phone calls made by the pastor epitomize and demonstrate the love and concern of God, and of the church. Such evidences of caring will be particularly valued by members of the baby boom generation, whose often harried lives are enriched by the personal contact of a pastor who takes time for them.

[1] "Baby Boomers: Boom or Bust for the Churches?", (*Progressions*, a Lilly Endowment Occasional Report. January,1990.)

[2] *Ibid.*

[3] *Ibid.*

[4] Jack Sims, "Baby Boomers: Time to Pass the Torch?" *Christian Life Magazine*. January, 1986. Cited in Hans Finzel, *Help! I'm A Baby Boomer* Wheaton: Victor Books, 1989, p. 143.

[5] Robert T.Gribbon, *Half the Congregation: Ministry With 18 to 40 Year Olds* (Washington: The Alban Institute, 1984), p. 21.

[6] Robert T. Gribbon, *Developing Faith In Young Adults* (Washington: The Alban Institute, 1990), p.56.

[7] *Ibid.,* p. 41.

[8] *The Boomer Report.* February, 1990.

[9] *Net Results.* September, 1989.

[10] A new church marketing resource kit has recently been developed and is available from Church Growth, Inc., 2670 So. Myrtle Ave. #201, Monrovia, CA. This kit includes sample newspaper ads, a radio "jingle," sample letters, etc. and can be helpful to a church communications committee.

[11] Lyle E. Schaller, "Twenty-One Steps to Reaching the Baby Boomers." *Net Results.* March, 1989.

[12] Wade Clark Roof, "The Church in the Centrifuge." *Christian Century*, November 8, 1989.

[13] *American Demographics.* August, 1988. p.57.

[14] Robert T. Gribbon, *When People Seek The Church.* Alban Institute Research Report. p. 17.

[15] Lyle E. Schaller, "New Baby Boom Is Predicted In '90s." *The Clergy Journal.* February, 1990.

[16] Gribbon, *Developing Faith In Young Adults*, p. 42.

[17] *Business Week*, September 25, 1989. See especially pages 145-148.

[18] Robert T. Gribbon, *Thirty Year Olds and the Church: Ministry with the Baby Boom Generation.* (Washington: The Alban Institute), p. 16.

[19] An excellent small group resource book has been written by Jeanne Hipp entitled, "How to Start & Grow Small Groups." available from Church Growth, Inc.

[20] Gribbon, *Developing Faith In Young Adults.* p. 43.

# Ministry Tasks Which Engage Baby Boomers

In the previous chapter, we directed our attention to specific ways in which a congregation can plan and carry out a ministry with the baby boom generation. Our purpose was to look at aspects of the church's ministry designed particularly to reach out to that group. Now we turn to those ministry areas common to most congregations, and consider how they may have a positive effect on the baby boom generation.

We have suggested that every church's ministry involves four fundamental tasks, or foundational pillars, which are worship, nurture, fellowship, and mission. Each pillar must be solid if the congregation is to have a strong and effective ministry. Each pillar must be substantial enough to support the concerns and needs of all the congregation's constituents, and none ought to appeal only to a single group within the congregation. Our purpose here is not to discuss all that these pillars ought to include, but rather to think about the ways they appear to baby boomers, and to discover what changes might be made in their design to make them most effective in ministry with that group.

## WORSHIP

Most of the people with whom a congregation is in active ministry will have their first contact with the church at a Sunday morning worship service. It is probable that this will be true for the majority of the baby boomers. The Sunday morning worship experience will form their first strong impressions of the congregation. Unless those impressions are positive, they will probably not return.

It is distressing to realize that the majority of first time worship visitors — of any age — do not return. According to the "Win Arn Growth Report," in the average American church only 12 to 15 percent of first time visitors return.[1] Even in growing churches, the average is only 20 to 25 percent. The highest rate of visitor return I have heard of falls below 50 percent.

Why do so many first time visitors fail to return? The primary reasons are either they did not feel welcome, or they were not satisfied with the service.

We have already spoken about the importance of a warm climate. It is hardly possible, however, to discuss the impact of the worship service without giving consideration to this issue. No matter how rich the quality of the worship, visitors are unlikely to return if they perceive the church to be cold and unfriendly. Most of us have had an experience in some commercial establishment in which we were quite satisfied with the product, but so unhappy with the way we were treated that we resolved never to return. The same kind of feelings and decisions occur every Sunday in thousands of churches throughout America.

As we consider the worship service itself, I realize we all have our ideas about how it should be done. Most of us probably prefer the way we worship in our own church. That is quite understandable. I think we would agree, however, that our preferences are mostly based on our own likes and dislikes. Few have theological significance. We need to be conscious of our prejudices as we explore worship that attracts and holds baby boomers.

The question I propose to discuss — and I want to put it as carefully as I can — is, "What kind of worship service is most likely to appeal to a baby boomer?" I know some people may believe that to be an improper question. Worship, they will say, is designed for God and should not be evaluated in terms of its appeal to any group of people. In an ultimate sense that may be true. Yet worship is an act performed by people, and surely God is pleased to have their number increase. If that is also true, it must be appropriate to reflect on ways in which that may happen. We will do that by looking first at some qualities of the worship service.

*Style.* Congregations effective in evangelization and experiencing numerical growth can be found among churches of every liturgical style. No one liturgical style seems to be most attractive. Any style done well will appeal to some baby boom people.

It is wise to plan, however, for variety within one's chosen style. Boring worship is one complaint consistently heard from baby boomers, and planned variety and innovation help conquer boredom. "Vital congregations build structured variety into worship," says Herb Miller, and they do it by "creatively varying the parts of a general format that remains the same each week." [2]

Whatever the liturgical style of worship, the service should be well-planned, and have unity. Everything should fit together and communicate a sense of connectedness. The service should flow, since there is movement in liturgy. The service should build to an appropriate conclusion, and enable worshipers to leave with the climax of the service fresh and empowering.

*Pace.* If the style of the worship service is not of vital importance, the pace is. A generation which grew up on television grows quickly impatient with a worship service which is slow and stodgy. It is most likely a slow pace, as much as anything else, that contributes to feelings of boredom. Baby boomers respond to a fast-paced worship service, and congregations who wish to reach them need to increase the tempo.

A number of factors affect the pace of worship. Music is surely one, and we will look at that in more detail shortly. The leaders of worship influence pace. Their enthusiasm, evidenced in facial expression, tone of voice, and speed of delivery, make a big difference, and so does what they say in leading worship. Few things slow down the pace more abruptly than hearing a worship leader repeat the announcement of a hymn three times, or make redundant comments, such as "Now let's all sing together." The pace of worship is enhanced by the participation of several worship leaders. I have found that people value being led in worship by several persons, including lay men and women.

One change necessary in congregations wishing to accelerate the pace of their service is to shorten some of the elements. Most people grow weary after singing five or six stanzas of a hymn. It helps to select appropriate verses, or to divide the hymn and sing parts of it at different times. Also, avoid long prayers. Several short ones are far better.

The total length of the service also should be considered. While for many Americans a one-hour service represents the standard, or even the absolute maximum length, that is not universally the case. In some of our cultures, much longer services are the rule. In either event the length of the service should conform to people's expectations. It should be recognized, however, that most baby boom visitors expect at most a one-hour service, and it is likely that a service which exceeds that length will discourage them from returning. Chances are that church members will overlook the occasional service that runs long, but visitors that day probably will not.

*Involvement.* Worship services that appeal to baby boomers are those which engage their experiences and emotions. Lyle Schaller says that "the fast-paced worship service that touches people at a feeling level and evokes a sense of active involvement in worship, as contrasted to a spectator rule" is most likely to attract younger generations. Schaller goes on to say "The intellectual approach to the faith wins fewer supporters today."[3] Worship which is celebrative and joyous has power.

*Atmosphere.* Mention should probably be made of baby boomers' apparent preference for informality, which has been noted as a characteristic of their generation. Evidence suggests that churches which manifest that quality are their preferred choice. Churches which communicate a relaxed environment appeal to them. That includes such matters as the informal dress of worshipers, a willingness to laugh or applaud in the service, a casual atmosphere, and a relaxed style.

Beyond these external characteristics are other issues of atmosphere. Worship that has meaning for the boom generation is one marked by a sense of the presence of God, and a corresponding climate of praise. Robert Gribbon, you may recall, gave as the first quality of congregations reaching the younger generation, that they are serious about their central religious task. [4] People go to church to be in touch with God. That is the primary need which the worship service must meet. God is the focal point of the service, and the whole atmosphere ought to be focused on "the vertical dimension" in which God is experienced and adored.

As God's presence is celebrated, the atmosphere evident will be one of grace. God draws near to people in love, seeking all,

154 THE MISSING GENERATION

welcoming, forgiving, embracing each. That is the good news which is made known in Jesus Christ. It is also made known in each service of worship as the congregation consistently acknowledges God's grace, joyfully responds with praise and thanksgiving, and displays love to all who are present. Baby boomers who may be attending their first service of worship should have a strong sense of the reality and depth of God's love and acceptance, as well as that of the congregation's.

## The Elements of Worship

We turn now to consider particular elements in the service, and begin by looking at features commonly found in worship services.

*Announcements.* My personal view is that announcements do not belong in the service. Announcements are an interruption of worship. They are experienced by many as boring and irrelevant. They insult people's intelligence if they repeat what can be read in a worship bulletin, and discourage the reading of that which has been prepared. When announcements are made — and sometimes they must be — they should be made for only one of two reasons: they call attention to an event of significance which is for *everyone*; or they make important information known which could not have been printed in the bulletin. Of course, church events do need to be promoted. But let the promotion be done by the group sponsoring the event, and avoid injecting promotion into the worship service.

*Children's Worship.* What about a children's sermon, or children's worship? My experience is that both children and parents benefit when children are brought to worship, and made to feel a part of it. In order to achieve both of those objectives, churches that desire to reach baby boom parents should accept the place of a children's sermon, though perhaps not every week. The practice of dismissing children from part of the regular service to attend children's worship also appeals to baby boom parents. It gives them freedom from distractions, and it fits with their value of each individual being given an opportunity for personal enrichment. Congregations in ministry to baby boomers will probably want to offer children's sermons and/or children's worship.

*Greeting Time.* In some congregations the worship service includes a time when people greet one another. I have seen no formal studies on how this practice is perceived by younger adults, and so offer only my personal observations. My experience is that baby boom visitors do not find this to be a positive experience. Fellowship cannot be forced, and shaking hands with a few strangers is not seen as very meaningful. If a greeting time lasts long enough to be valuable to members it will probably create a feeling of discomfort in visitors. It seems preferable for the pastor to give a warm verbal welcome to visitors, and for members to personally greet and welcome them informally before and after the service.

*Sharing Time.* A practice which seems to be increasingly popular, however, is a time during worship for the sharing of joys and concerns. This is usually followed by a prayer of intercession. Such a time can be a very meaningful experience which personifies and validates a congregation's love and concern. It is most meaningful to members, but visitors appreciate it, as well. Some risk exists in that sometimes a person shares more than is desirable and causes embarrassment.

*The Sermon.* The main elements of worship to be considered are the sermon and the music. Let's look at the sermon first. Lyle Schaller reports that he has asked several thousand new members why they joined a particular congregation. He indicates that "younger adults usually begin their response by praising the preaching, the meaningful content of the sermons, and the communication skills of the preacher." Schaller concludes, "It is difficult to overstate the power of good preaching today, and it is usually the number one factor in determining where the baby boomers go to church."[5]

The first requirement of sermons that attract the young adults of the baby boom is that they be clearly biblical. Herb Miller declares that baby boomers "respond far more positively to 'Biblical' preaching than the generation immediately preceding them. These young adults define a biblical sermon as one that contains a high percentage of biblical content. They expect the central point of the sermon to grow out of the biblical text itself, instead of developing as a philosophical point with a biblical text thrown in as an illustration." [6]

Baby boomers also expect sermons that are practical. It is not enough that the sermon clearly sets forth biblical truth. Of equal importance is that the truth be applied to everyday life. Sermons which are valued relate to the issues with which they are dealing, and have a "how to" focus. Baby boomers are deeply interested in personal growth and self-improvement. Practical messages reach them.

The sermons they value are also personal. They are personal in that they clearly arise out of the life of the preacher. This is apparent not so much in the illustrations which may be used, but in the evidence that the speaker is also living and perhaps struggling with the issue being dealt with. The humanity, as well as the personality, of the preacher must come through. The sermon is also personal in that it makes a personal appeal. It challenges attitudes and feelings and calls for an individual response. Sermons preferred by baby boomers are not orations or lectures, but are those of a conversational style.

*The Music.* The second major area of the worship service to be considered is the music. During the last few years, I have visited a number of the churches in this country which are reaching large groups of baby boomers. I found more differences between them than I expected, but I was impressed by one thing all of them had in common. They all make extensive use of contemporary music.

Before describing this further, let me be clear about my own musical tastes. My preference is classical music, and my experience has mostly been in churches which feature that style. I was surprised to learn that only 6 percent of the American public indicates classical music as their preference. There are a lot of churches gearing their music to a rather small slice of the population. I would hazard a guess that most of the churches which feature predominantly classical music are not experiencing numerical growth and are not reaching baby boomers in significant numbers. That leads me to rethink my own views on this subject.

It is difficult to overestimate the importance music has had — and still has — to the baby boom. They have, after all, been called the "Rock Generation." Jack Sims writes of his fellow baby boomers: "Except for our age, our passionate acceptance of a similar style of music is the most common denominator of our generation. This shared preference for up-tempo music . . . is a very significant thread which binds us together. We all like to hear and feel the sound." [7]

That was certainly evident in the churches I visited. A common pattern is that hymn books are nowhere in evidence, and neither organ or piano is used. Some kind of musical group with guitars, drums, synthesizers and "what have you" accompanies the singing. And they sing a lot in these

churches.    Words  to  contemporary  songs
appear on large screens, and people sing.

During these times of singing, I began to
notice several things.  Just about all the songs
have been written in the life time of even the
youngest baby boomer.  The words of the songs
are usually taken from the Bible, or they are
addressed directly to God, as opposed to talking
about God.    The music is easy to sing, and
some of the melodies are hauntingly beautiful.
The younger generation loves to sing it, and the
singing both evokes and expresses emotion.  It
has  power.    I  found  myself  moved  by  it,
beginning to sing it, and worshiping through
it. I wanted to take some of the joy and power it
produced to share with some churches which
have not tasted much of either lately.

Contemporary music is a very important
component in a worship service attractive to
the baby boom, and churches reaching them
use  a  good  deal  of  it.    Schaller  encourages
churches to use between two and five pieces of
special musical at each worship service.[8]

Some who read this will be members of
fairly traditional congregations.   You may
want to reach the baby boom, but the music in
your  congregation  is  a  long  way  from
contemporary.  What can you do?  I would not
immediately assume that nothing can be done.
People are not likely to stand up and applaud if
they show up next Sunday to discover that the
organ has been replaced by a rock band.  Yet it
is possible to introduce some of this music in
ways that may be beneficial.

Introducing  change  is  always  easier
when the reason for it is known, and when the

change is seen as provisional. That suggests letting people know in advance what is being proposed, why it is believed important, and the length of time the change will be in effect. One possible method involves informing the congregation of the purpose behind this plan and then indicating that for a three month period the service will begin with ten minutes of singing contemporary songs, perhaps with instrumental accompaniment. People may discover they like this, and want to continue it. Thus a permanent feature of worship can offer music of different types to meet the needs of different generations present in worship.

*Additional or Alternate Services.* A second option which may actually be both easier to introduce and more effective in reaching a significant number of boomers, is to add an additional worship service especially for these persons. This approach has much to commend it. Research has confirmed that adding a second service nearly always increases the total number of worship participants, particularly when the two services are different. Schaller identifies this as "one of the most effective tactics in a larger strategy" to reach young adults.[9] Schaller also suggests that, in most cases, the earlier Sunday morning service should be the one planned for the younger crowd.

   In a number of churches involved in ministry with this generation, worship services are offered at times other than Sunday morning. The most common alternatives are a Thursday evening or a Saturday evening service. The appeal of such a service is partially in its evidence of willingness to accommodate to the concerns of those the church is seeking to evangelize. An added benefit is the complete freedom one has in designing the style, content, and format of a new event. No one can find fault with its design, since no one knows what a Saturday evening service is supposed to look like.

Every congregation is always making decisions about its worship. Those interested in reaching baby boomers will be prepared to evaluate and alter their worship (or add an additional service) in order to be effective in reaching the baby boom generation.

## NURTURE

One of the crucial tasks of the church is to help people grow spiritually. Nurture is a good word to describe that task, for it means "to further the development of." Nurturing occurs particularly through a congregation's educational ministry. This ministry is also an important avenue for reaching the baby boom. "A strong teaching ministry is an almost universal characteristic of those congregations attracting large numbers of younger adults. Many of those born before 1956 place this on the same level as preaching as a reason for choosing this church." [10]

There is no doubt about the baby boom's interest in education. These persons are committed to life-long learning, and many are as eager to continue to learn for themselves as they are committed to their children's education. Churches in ministry with the baby boom need to provide quality educational experiences in both adult and children's education. In his book *Pursuing Excellence In Ministry,* Daniel Biles identifies quality education as one key expression of excellence in ministry. "It is aimed at seeing that members, especially adults, are biblically and theologically literate in order that they might know what it means to be Christians in today's world and witness effectively."[11]

Children's education is certainly a key to providing an opportunity for initial ministry with baby boom families. Robert Gribbon reports that "both churched and unchurched parents say they want religious education for their children."[12] Churches that make quality children's education available will find a ready market. A congregation in New Jersey has developed an excellent children's education ministry. News of this has gotten around by word of mouth and people have called from as far as twenty-five miles away seeking to enroll their children in the program.

Adult education is an even greater opportunity. The primary focus of the church's educational program for adults should center in providing spiritual growth. Baby boom people think of life in terms of a journey, and it is the church which must provide food for the journey. Many baby boomers have a deep interest in studying the Bible and learning how it relates to life. One young woman expressed a common sentiment when she said, "I don't have any interest in learning the names of the twelve disciples, but

I have great desire to understand how the Bible relates to my life." Education needs to assist adults in their relationship with God and their understanding of God's work in the world today.

It would be helpful to suggest a few ideas for churches wanting to make their educational program effective and attractive to the baby boom generation. First, adult classes should be *organized around interest areas* and not by age groupings or marital status. This is a good general rule which may be broken occasionally to offer brief classes designed for particular groups, such as a course for newlyweds on marriage. Second, *a variety of classes* is important. Among other advantages, this allows the church to make provision for people who are at different levels of development, and allows for both introductory and advanced classes. Third, *quality is crucial*, and that means qualified, trained, prepared teachers, as well as up-to-date resources, materials, and equipment. If you must choose between quantity and quality, choose quality. Fourth, all classes need to be encouraged to *bring in new people*. Lyle Schaller says that in an ideal class, 5 to 10% of the group will have begun participating during the past year.[13] Fifth, recognize that the pastor or pastors can be very effective by teaching *classes for people exploring or beginning affiliation* with the church. Christian education specialists point out the importance of the commitment, enthusiasm, and the visible leadership of the pastor in the church's education ministry. And through the pastor's teaching of "entry event" classes, significant results can be expected. Sixth, *start new classes* regularly. Charles Arn, in the book *Growth: A New Vision for the Sunday School,* observes that most classes "saturate" within two years and stop growing. And that the best response to this natural pattern is to regularly start new classes.[14] A goal should be to begin at least one new class each year.

When a new class or group begins, it ordinarily draws its membership from the ranks of those not currently involved in an educational class. That means new classes reach more people. New classes and groups are also more effective in encouraging the participation of new members. Many newcomers hesitate to join existing groups because such groups feel "closed" to them. New classes reach more new people. New classes also provide an opportunity to explore issues and themes not presently being addressed in a congregation's educational program. They provide a positive response to emerging needs. New groups broaden choices by offering options.

Recently, a survey was taken of congregations in the Reformed Church which have experienced the greatest numerical growth over the past decade. All but one of the churches reported a growing Sunday school enrollment. Clearly, evangelization and education are closely linked.

## FELLOWSHIP

All congregations have an interest in fellowship, and a correct desire that it occur within their church family. After all, Christianity is about relationships, and facilitating relationships is one way to describe the church's task. While all congregations desire fellowship, not all make an effort to evaluate how well fellowship is occuring in their church, or have intentional plans to strengthen it. Congregations eager for an effective ministry with the baby boom, however, will do both.

The desire for a place to belong, a search for intimacy, and a hunger for friendships are all factors in the lives of significant numbers of baby boomers. Quality fellowship in the church provides an opportunity to respond to all of these needs.

Usually some degree of fellowship occurs whenever the congregation gathers. Fellowship can be enhanced, however, when intentional provision is made for it. Many churches now being constructed plan large lobby areas where conversations can take place after a service or event. In some church buildings, space is limited which will require some compensatory action. Generally, when conversations continue well after the con-clusion of an event, it is an indication of a church in which fellowship is strong, but that is not always true. A more important indication is whether newcomers are regularly included in these conversational groups.

The "coffee hour" after a worship service provides a great socializing opportunity. It's effectiveness increases when:  a) it is held in a main traffic area;  b) an invitation in the church bulletin each week encourages everyone, specifically visitors, to attend;  c) people in the church intentionally invite and escort newcomers to the coffee area and introduce them to others; and,  d) a variety of refreshments are available.

Fellowship is experienced primarily through smaller groups which are part of the congregation's life.  Adult classes, choirs, small groups, athletic events, Bible studies, special interest activities, ministry groups — whenever a group gathers, fellowship occurs. Fellowship is often experienced around tasks, and when church groups gather, one is often struck by the depth of fellowship.  That warm enjoyment of others needs to be experienced by newcomers as well.

Classes and groups in the church increase their potential to attract baby boomers when they make a special effort to reach and include newcomers from that generation. Regularly scheduling social events is one way to achieve that, especially if the purpose is to also invite guests.  Another way is to work at tasks which bring new people into the group. Some groups have an organized system for incorporating newcomers, and making contact with absent members.  Within the groups, opportunity must be given for people to share their needs and stories.  Groups and classes are the primary way in which the fellowship of the church is experienced.

Athletic activities and programs can form an important "port of entry" for congregations seeking to reach baby boomers. Some churches sponsor a variety of sports teams, or even entire leagues, and encourage the recruitment of people outside the church. Groups which include both men and women are particularly effective. Special events like a golf outing, volleyball night, or a party involving swimming or bowling are attractive events. Activities like these are wonderful opportunities for inviting, and are the easiest invitations to extend and accept. The intention is that, by meeting people from the church, those who do not belong will be attracted by the warmth and welcome of church people and join them in other experiences for which they come together. Fellowship can be both an entry event and a response to an ongoing need.

## MISSION

Congregations which are pursuing a clearly defined ministry plan are churches in mission. Much of what they do is directly related to their goal of evangelization, and everything they do is evaluated in light of that purpose. This does not mean that everything they do is designed to win converts, but the central purpose of "disciple-making" is always a point of evaluation for success.

Mission is an important concern to many people in the baby boom generation, and congregations reaching them are those which give evidence of God's love through their caring service to others in need. In his study on excellence in ministry, David Biles placed mission as the highest indicator. In the churches Biles surveyed, he found that "what was present in all of these churches was a strong emphasis and understanding of mission, fueled by a set of values which encapsulated the congregation's understanding of its mission and provided the motivating power for doing the tasks of ministry."[15] The Biles' study points out that a renewed and focused mission has the power to transform declining churches.

Strengthening the pillar of mission may take place in a variety of ways. It may begin with a discussion group which focuses on a social concern and explores opportunities to respond. It may start as a response to a community crisis or need. Perhaps it begins when a group from the congregation participates in a mission project, or a tour of some mission field. It may arise out of a congregation's history of giving generous financial support to world mission causes, or develop when new leaders articulate a vision for mission.

When a congregation is strong in mission, in all likelihood that strength will be apparent in four ways. First, the congregation works at "mission education," sponsoring forums or classes which help provide understanding regarding social issues and mission concerns. Second, the congregation gives regular and generous financial support for mission needs and projects. Third, the congregation has a clear understanding of, and commitment to mission in its immediate community. Fourth, the congregation deploys ministry groups which are actively involved in doing ministry within the community.

Perhaps that last characteristic is the most crucial. Great numbers of baby boom people, including those whose social consciences were honed by the events of the 1960s, want very much to respond to the social needs of our world. They are eager to learn about these problems, but not satisfied to simply understand them. They want an opportunity to do something which can make a difference, and they want to work at tasks which have meaning for their lives. Congregations which provide opportunities for their members to work with the homeless, provide meals for the hungry, get involved in a prison ministry, or participate in some such project are churches which appeal to baby boomers who want to serve.

And many do want to serve. In spite of their busy schedules, 48 percent of Americans do volunteer work. Cheryl Russell observes that "these volunteers donate an average of eighteen hours a month of their time, and most of that goes to churches."[16] Russell expects volunteerism to increase among baby boomers because the highest proportion of volunteers are people in the 35 to 49 age bracket. The oldest boomers are more than half-way into that age group and volunteering is highest among college graduates, which represent about one-quarter of the baby boom.

Volunteerism is on the increase in the baby boom. Churches which provide meaningful, challenging opportunities for people in their generation to be in mission, will see volunteers coming forward.

Worship, nurture, fellowship, mission: each has drawing power. As a congregation gives consideration to these pillars of effective ministry, it will want to identify how each would look if it were to be attractive to the baby boom, and then make decisions about what changes it is willing to introduce.

[1] "Win Arn Growth Report" #28 (Monrovia: Church Growth, Inc.).

[2] Herb Miller, *The Vital Congregation* (Nashville: Abingdon Press, 1990).

[3] Lyle E. Schaller, "Twenty-One Steps To Reaching The Baby-Boomers" *Net Results*, March, 1989.

[4] Robert T. Gribbon, *1/2 The Congregation: Ministry With 18 to 40 Year Olds* (Washington: The Alban Institute, 1984), p. 28.

[5] Schaller, "Twenty-One Steps."

[6] Miller, *The Vital Congregation.* p. 38.

[7] Jack Sims, "The Baby Boom Church" *Church Business Report.* (Fax Unlimited, Inc., 1983.)

[8] Schaller, "Twenty-One Steps," *op. cit.*

[9] Lyle E. Schaller, *Choices for Churches*, (Nashville: Abingdon Press, 1990), p. 87.

[10] Schaller, "Twenty-One Steps."

[11] Daniel V. Biles, *Pursuing Excellence In Ministry* (Washington: The Alban Institute, 1988), p. 9.

[12] Robert T. Gribbon, *Thirty Year Olds and the Church: Ministry with the Baby Boom Generation* (Washington: The Alban Institute, 1981), p. 16.

[13] Lyle E. Schaller, "Why Offer Adult Classes?" *The Parish Paper.* June, 1989.

[14] Charles Arn, *Growth: A New Vision for the Sunday School.* (Monrovia: Church Growth Press, 1980), p. 103.

[15] Biles, *Pursuing Excellence in Ministry.*

[16] Cheryl Russell, *100 Predictions For the Baby Boom.* (New York: Plenum Press, 1987), p. 142.

# CHAPTER NINE

# Getting Started

In an important study of mainline Protestantism, Roof and McKinney speak about a new spirit with which the church must contend: "Of all the recent religious changes in America, few are more significant, or more subtle, than the enhanced religious individualism of our time... Religion is highly voluntary in contemporary America — a matter ultimately of personal choice and conscience."[1]

One obvious consequence of religious individualism is a "consumer attitude" toward church involvement. That is, people make choices about church on the basis of whether it meets their needs and satisfies their desires. *Fortune* magazine featured an article on the theme "Turning around the Lord's Business."[2] The article set out to answer the question of why one church thrives while another struggles. The explanation the article offers is "success comes to those who best serve their flock." Without getting into a discussion as to whether "success" is an appropriate goal for a church, it can be recognized that congregations which provide "customer satisfaction" are going to be most effective in reaching people. This will be particularly true of reaching baby boom people, who are the most likely to search for, and insist on, personal satisfaction.

Without question, there is an unhealthy aspect to this consumer mentality. It is, to be honest, selfishness, and no church wants to cater to that. It can also lead churches down dangerous paths in their efforts to "succeed." The *Fortune* article offers as a formula for success: "to find a need the competition is not meeting." Something in that goes against the spirit and teaching of Jesus Christ. Churches are not, or ought not be, in the business of competing.

Having recognized that, the question is, What is the church to do? Probably not much can be done about "religious individualism," although perhaps the teaching ministries of the church can make some impact by exploring the spiritual issues involved. In terms of pursuing ministry, the choice seems to be between refusing to play the game, and therefore not getting involved in attempting to offer "customer service," or recognizing the "market place" reality and trying to respond with the goal of reaching them for Christ and his church. I opt for the second alternative, but with the hope that the game will be played non-competitively, with grace and compassion. Now, how might we begin?

*Develop a Conviction in the Congregation*
*About the Need to Reach the Baby Boom*

In a lecture on reaching for the baby boom, Tex Sample, a professor at the St. Paul School of Theology in Kansas City, said the place to get started is by developing a conviction in the congregation that this is a "field ripe for harvest." Developing such a conviction flows out of the evangelizing vision of the congregation. Those who come to believe in the priority and opportunity of that task are not likely to think 30 million unchurched baby boomers can be ignored.

More than conviction, however, is involved in successfully reaching baby boomers. It requires agreement that, as a church, a special effort to reach that generation is both legitimate and necessary. Further, as that conviction is being developed, the congregation must come to terms with the implications and major changes in church life and programs which will be required if a ministry effort is to be effective. Inevitably, that will lead people to question the effort. One can expect to encounter an attitude which asks why the congregation should cater to the baby boom generation.

To give an example, let's consider what happened in one church. The pastor proposed beginning a contemporary Thursday evening worship service to reach the baby boomers. When the proposal was introduced, mention was made about the frequency with which this generation goes away for the weekend, and that Sunday is increasingly seen as the day for the family to do something together. It was pointed out that these factors keep many baby boomers from attending the Sunday service.

Some church members immediately objected. They resented "caving in" as one person put it, to what they saw as an abandonment of the concept of the Lord's Day for worship, and condoning a hedonistic spirit in the missing group. They saw the proposal of the Thursday evening service as contrary to what the church stood for, and could not bring themselves to support the plan.

Differences like these need to be openly discussed. It is always right for the church to make possible a fair and honest sharing of differences. In some cases, those differences will be deep, and may not be fully resolved, but they do need to be addressed.

One possible approach in this case is to help members of the congregation understand that many missing baby boomers are daughters and sons of the church. Indeed, one suspects that not a few of the congregation's older members may themselves have children among those who have left the church. It is important to help such persons deal with their pain, guilt, and anger about that situation. We may all grieve that the church has been unable to be the way to wholeness for so many. We all share, in part, responsibility for the church's shortcomings, because we are a community. It helps to admit that.

This approach makes it possible for all of us to share in the efforts of ministry with this generation. The issue to explore with the church family is this: What are we willing to give to bring them back? Might it be appropriate, for example, that reference be made to John 3:16 and then ask what we are willing to give to reach the missing generation?

A ministry plan will often require major changes in a church if that church is to reach the world. Those changes will create conflict. When conflict occurs, it must be faced and dealt with. Conflict over the issues we have discussed will be reduced by the approach suggested.

It has been my observation that when a church is providing ministry which meets the needs of its present members, there is greater openness to new ventures in ministry. When older members, for example, find the preaching and teaching ministry of the congregation facilitating their spiritual journey, when they are receiving meaningful fellowship and care, and are given opportunities for personal involvement in ministry, they are likely to be supportive of (or at least tolerant of) special efforts to reach younger adults. Tex Sample is right. Ministry with the baby boom begins by developing a conviction in the congregation of the need for it.

## *Gather a Group to Evaluate and Plan*

Getting started in a ministry with the baby boom begins by making use of the present members of the congregation who are part of that group. It has been suggested that one approach might be to gather a group of the congregation's 25 to 45-year-old members to discuss ministry with the baby boomers. A session could be planned in which the issues are raised and the possibility of a ministry focus addressed. The group might identify one or two program areas which could be addressed and offer suggestions for further steps to be taken. Perhaps some in the group will volunteer to serve on a task force to work on further plans and decisions.

Another option is to invite people from the baby boom generation who have joined the congregation within the past two years to come together for an evening of "focus groups."

A focus group is a gathering of people who have something specifically in common with each other and are brought together to discuss that common area. The invitation to attend this one-time gathering identifies the common area, and asks people to share their experiences and attitudes in that area, making clear why this information is needed and what will be done with it. A focus group is designed to learn from those people whose experience make them the best source of understanding. Questions are usually prepared in advance, and the convener of the group is responsible to help participants express their feelings so that as much information as possible is obtained. A focus group is not a discussion group, so the leader must be sure that people's ideas are not debated, but rather their experiences and opinions are simply stated.

The focus group plan suggested here involves gathering the younger and newer members of the congregation to explore the process of entry into the church, and specifically what helps and what hinders that process. Sample questions might include:

- The first time you attended here, what brought you?
- What led you to make a return visit?
- Can you identify people in the congregation who made you feel welcome?
- In which groups or activities of the congregation are you currently participating?
- If you were to bring a friend to a worship service here, what would you be concerned about?
- Now that you have been here for a time, what have you seen that you think might be important to share?

Gribbon adds the following questions:

1. What first attracted you to this congregation? What helped your transition into this particular congregation?
2. What almost stopped you from involvement in this congregation? What are the problems for you in this congregation? What turns you off?
3. What holds you here? Where are the places your needs are met? What draws you into deeper involvement?
4. What advice do you have for this congregation?[3]

Scheduling such a "talk it over" session with baby boom members is a way of gathering important information from the recent personal experiences of those who know your congregation. Such information is invaluable.

Immediately following this information gathering exercise, put in writing the information which emerges. Test your findings with participants and ask them to read the report to be sure the information is accurate and complete. Any new feedback should be reflected in a rewriting of the report, which may then be submitted to the task force working on the congregation's ministry plan.

*Create a Plan for Evangelizing*

Getting started in a ministry with the baby boom generation involves developing an evangelizing plan.

The most effective process of evangelization arises out of the existing relationships between members of the congregation and friends, family, and associates who are not part of the church. An indispensable ingredient in an evangelism plan involves encouraging and equipping church members for "relational evangelism." If that is to occur, church members must be helped to identify people with whom they can be in ministry, discover how to relate to them in such a way that love and caring will be evident, and learn how and when to appropriately speak of their faith. In addition, church members need the opportunity to interact with other members involved in similar efforts so that support and accountability may be provided. An excellent resource entitled, "The Master's Plan Church Action Kit" has been produced by Church Growth, Inc. which offers a helpful approach to achieving the above objectives. [4]

A second ingredient in an evangelizing plan is a process of visitor follow-up. A congregation intent on reaching baby boomers needs to have an effective method for obtaining the names and addresses of worship visitors, and then initiate follow-up contacts. In a study of growing Reformed churches, more than 86 percent of the fastest growing churches had an intentional follow-up plan for visitors.

Follow-up of first-time visitors is especially important. Strategies vary, but it is universally recognized by church growth authorities that responses to first-time visitors must take place promptly, and that lay persons are most effective in making them. Lay persons' contacts seem to be preferred by unchurched persons because they have no professional involvement in the church and are not likely to be perceived as acting out of self-interest (i.e. "They are paid to do this"). An effective strategy being used in some congregations is that a lay person telephones first-time visitors the afternoon or evening of their visit to thank them for coming and invite them to return. These are usually brief conversations that include a comment from the callers about an aspect or quality of the congregation they find personally meaningful.

A third component in an effective evangelism plan is to develop and work with a "responsibility list" — a record of the names of those whom the church is seeking to evangelize. The names of recent church visitors may be on the responsibility list, as well as those persons who have had some contact with the congregation during the past two years. It is wise to plan a method of making regular contact with people on the responsibility list. A series of specially prepared mailings may be sent over a period of time. Periodic phone conversations may take place inviting such persons to a special event, offering a service, or simply communicating concern. Occasionally, an offer to stop by and tell them more about the church is appropriate. [5] Whatever specific strategy is designed, a responsibility list is an excellent way of identifying and maintaining contact with the people a congregation is seeking to evangelize.

A fourth component in an evangelization plan for baby boomers involves providing opportunities for people to learn more about the Christian faith, the denomination of which the church is a part, and the heritage of that particular church. Many baby boomers who begin exploring affiliation with the church come with very little understanding of these areas. They may have little or no knowledge of the Bible or the Christian faith. Their exposure to a church, if there has been one, will probably have occurred in a different denominational group. Given baby boomers' commitment to education and hunger for information, learning opportunities in the areas mentioned are of significant value. An added benefit is that, as people go through such learning experiences, they are able to make informed decisions about commitment and be bonded to the congregation.

One obvious method of providing such learning is for the church to periodically offer classes on such subjects as basic Christian beliefs, and/or what this congregation believes. If the church is part of a denomination, it may offer a class which acquaints people with it. Periodically, a class might be offered on the life and ministry opportunities of the congregation. Classes such as these have an appeal to members, as well as to those exploring affiliation.

Lyle Schaller suggests additional steps which might be taken to help people understand and value the heritage and identity of the church and denomination. Possibilities include a visit to denominational ministries, to a college or seminary of the church, or a tour of denominational/regional offices. Other suggestions include preparing and distributing a history of the church, conducting a trip to the church's mission fields, or to Israel to study the historical lands of the Bible, arranging a work-camp experience, a celebration of the congregation's anniversary with a video telling the story of the church's life and ministry over the past twelve months, or some variation of these ideas.[6]

Developing a plan for evangelization also requires consideration of a pre-membership class. Making such a class a prerequisite to membership is desirable, and may actually make membership more meaningful. A primary purpose of a membership class is *relational* — not instructional — as bonds are formed both with people in the joining process and with the congregation's pastor and leaders. However, the class does provide an excellent opportunity to deal with the issue of commitment, both in terms of commitment to Jesus Christ and to the congregation.

Commitment does not come easily for many people in the baby boom generation, but a time must come when those contemplating membership are helped to understand clearly what commitment means and involves and are challenged to make their own commitments. Evangelizing congregations will want to provide that opportunity for all who explore membership by making the issues of commitment clear and providing an environment in which people can make freely chosen decisions.

## A REVIEW OF WHERE WE'VE COME

Charles Kraft once wrote: "Established Christianity has often feared to alter the forms lest in doing so the content be lost. By so doing, however, it has unwittingly assured that the content would largely be lost. The dynamic of Christianity, however, is not in the sacredness of cultural forms . . . [but] in the venturesomeness of participating with God in the transformation of contemporary cultural forms to serve more adequately as vehicles for God's interactions with human beings." [7]

We have advocated adopting evangelization as a priority for the congregation, encouraging ministry with the baby boom as a primary focus of that evangelization, and developing a ministry plan to reach this "missing generation." We have urged a congregation to recognize that efforts to reach that generation will mean major changes in the life of a congregation and have pointed out the importance of helping people in the church understand that necessity and be willing to work at implementing change.

We have suggested an open approach to the baby boom generation which includes adapting to their needs and interests, going to them, and also inviting them to participate in the life of the church. We looked at ways to encourage their participation and stressed the importance of being a welcoming and hospitable community. We suggested providing an opportunity for baby boomers to come in through a variety of open doors so that they can understand what the Christian faith is all about, what this congregation is and does, and still walk back out if that is their choice.

We have proposed that a congregation develop specific program ventures designed to respond to interests, concerns, and needs of the baby boom, and that these events be communicated by both promotion and personal invitation. We discussed looking at the various ministries of the church to see how they might appeal to the baby boom and advocated making changes to increase their attractiveness.

Underlying all of this has been the assumption that evangelization — the fundamental task of the church — is not just a matter of words but calls us to understand and love people and to provide ministry opportunities appropriate to their needs and interests so that the good news they see and hear will make them want to respond.

Our model and pattern is Jesus Christ. As I think about our Lord's ministry, I am constantly reminded of the fact that in dealing with people, even "the sinners" of his time, Jesus never began by dealing with their sin. Beginning there is more likely to close doors than to open them. Certainly that is true in ministry with baby boomers. The themes of sin and forgiveness are not appropriate avenues of approach, since many of them do not feel much guilt and are not motivated by it. A better approach can be found.

Recall the wonderful story of Jesus and Zacchaeus (Luke 19:1-10). On all the evidence, Zacchaeus was a traitor and a crook. Yet Jesus' approach to him was pure grace. A lot of us got the song wrong in Sunday School. We had Jesus looking up into the sycamore tree and saying, "Zacchaeus, you come down," in a tone of sharp rebuke, with his finger pointing skyward. It couldn't have been that way at all. Those words were spoken by one whose face shone with delight, and whose arms were open wide with welcome, the way a person greets a great friend. It was that which brought Zacchaeus leaping from the tree in joy and wonder.

We are not told what they talked about during the dinner at Zacchaeus' house. Perhaps the reason is that what Jesus *did* that day in Jericho was more important than the conversation that followed. We do know that during that evening, a transformed Zacchaeus said some amazing things about the changes he would be making in his life.

This incident, and others like it in the Gospels, are great models for our ministry with the generation of baby boomers. I am not going to belabor the points which are obvious, but I do want to make one final observation. Many of us were taught that in order for people to become Christians, two steps are required: repentance (turning from sin), and faith (turning to God). So, indeed I believe. For much of my life I assumed that those steps were taken in that order — first one repented, and then one believed.

The story of Zacchaeus suggests a different possible order — in fact, just the opposite. No doubt Zacchaeus knew he was a sinner even before he met Jesus. What he did not know, or could not believe, was that God knew him as he was, and loved him deeply. It was Jesus' behavior with Zacchaeus that helped Zacchaeus understand that God believed in him. That is what melted his heart. It enabled him to believe in God, and that led to repentance.

Here, it seems to me, is a model for ministry with the baby boomers: to let them know God loves them by the ways in which we love them, to illustrate God's acceptance of them by our own acceptance, to demonstrate God's gift by our own giving. The theme we need to lift up and celebrate to touch their hearts is the theme of grace. The point we want to highlight is that in God's family you can come home again. That needs to be said frequently and clearly, but most of all it needs to be shown — by our open arms, and homes, and churches.

The spiritual journey of the baby boom generation is not over, but the coming decade will go a long way toward indicating how many of the "missing generation" will be found. Who we are and what we do in the church is the determining factor.

[1] Wade Clark Roof and William McKinney, *American Mainline Religion*, (New Brunswick: Rutgers University Press, 1987), pp. 40, 43.

[2] *Fortune.* September 25, 1989.

[3] Robert T. Gribbon, *Developing Faith in Young Adults.* (Washington: The Alban Institute, 1990), pp. 86, 87.

[4] The kit is available from Church Growth, Inc., Monrovia, California.

[5] A helpful approach to prospect acquisition and follow-up has been developed by Church Growth, Inc., entitled "The Caring System." A catalog describing this resource and others is available upon request by calling 1-818-447-2112.

[6] Lyle E. Schaller, *Choices for Churches*, (Nashville: Abingdon Press, 1990), p. 89.

[7] Charles H. Kraft, *Christianity in Culture*, (Maryknoll, NY: Orbis Books, 1979), p. 382.

# BIBLIOGRAPHY

Anderson, Leith. *Dying For Change.* Minneapolis: Bethany Book Publishers, 1990.

Arn, Win. *The Church Growth Ratio Book.* Monrovia: Church Growth, Inc. 1988.

Barna, George. *Marketing The Church.* Colorado Springs: NavPress, 1988.

Bast, Robert L. *Attracting New Members.* Monrovia: Church Growth, Inc., 1988.

Biles, Daniel V. *Pursuing Excellence in Ministry. Washington: The Alban Institute, 1988.*

Bellah, Mike. *Baby Boom Believers.* Wheaton: Tyndale House, 1988.

Finzel, Hans. *Help! I'm A Baby Boomer.* Wheaton: Victor Books, 1989.

Gribbon, Robert T. *Developing Faith In Young Adults.* The Alban Institute, 1990.

Hadaway, Wright, and Dubowns. *Home Cell Groups and House Churches.* Nashville: Broadman Press, 1987.

Jones, Landon Y. *Great Expectations: America and the Baby Boom.* New York: Random House, 1980.

Light, Paul C. *Baby Boomers.* New York: W.W. Norton and Company, 1988.

Miller, Herb. *The Vital Congregation.* Nashville: Abingdon Press, 1990.

Mueller, White. *Direct Mail Ministry.* Nashville: Abingdon Press, 1989.

Roof, Wade Clark, and McKinney, William. *American Mainline Religion: Its Changing Shape and Future.* New Brunswick: Rutgers University Press, 1987.

Russell, Cheryl. *100 Predictions For The Baby Boom.* New York: Plenum Press, 1987.

Schaller, Lyle E. *Choices For Churches.* Nashville: Abingdon Press, 1990.

Yankelovich. *New Rules.* New York: Random House, 1981.